Ohio DMV Exam Workbook:

Your Essential Guide to the Ohio Driving Test

Master the Ohio DMV Exam with the Best Ohio Driver's Practice Tests

Introduction

The Ohio DMV Exam Workbook is a comprehensive guide designed to help individuals prepare for and pass the Ohio driving test. The driving test is a critical step in obtaining a driver's license in Ohio, and it is essential to be well-prepared to pass. This workbook is valuable for anyone seeking to become a safe and responsible driver on Ohio's roads.

The driving test assesses a driver's knowledge of Ohio's traffic laws, road signs, and safe driving practices. It is important to thoroughly understand these concepts to pass the test and become a licensed driver in Ohio. The Ohio DMV Exam Workbook provides readers with a comprehensive overview of these topics and offers practice tests to help them assess their understanding.

The Ohio DMV Exam Workbook is organized into several sections, each covering a specific aspect of driving in Ohio. The first section covers the basics of driving, including information on Ohio's traffic laws, road signs, and safe driving practices. The subsequent sections cover more advanced topics, such as driving in hazardous conditions and defensive driving techniques.

In addition to the comprehensive coverage of driving topics, the Ohio DMV Exam Workbook includes a range of practice tests. These tests are designed to mimic the Ohio driving test, allowing readers to assess their knowledge and identify areas where they need to improve. The practice tests are an invaluable resource for anyone preparing to take the driving test, as they provide a realistic experience of what to expect on the exam day.

One of the key benefits of the Ohio DMV Exam Workbook is its accessibility. The book is written clearly and concisely, making it easy for readers to understand the information presented. The practice tests are also well-designed and easy to follow, allowing readers to track their progress and identify areas where they may need additional study.

Another benefit of the Ohio DMV Exam Workbook is its emphasis on defensive driving techniques. The book provides practical advice on how to anticipate and avoid potential hazards on the road, which is essential for becoming a safe and responsible driver. The emphasis on defensive driving sets the Ohio DMV Exam Workbook apart from other driving test resources. It makes it an essential read for anyone serious about becoming a safe and responsible driver.

Overall, the Ohio DMV Exam Workbook is an essential guide for anyone preparing to take the Ohio driving test. Its comprehensive coverage of driving topics, practical advice, and range of practice tests provides readers with everything they need to know to pass the test and become a safe and responsible drivers. The following chapters will give a more detailed overview of the book's content and how it can help individuals achieve their goal of becoming licensed drivers in Ohio.

Table of Contents

Traffic laws and signs   1

This includes knowledge of Ohio's traffic laws, as well as understanding how to interpret and follow traffic signs and signals.

Traffic laws and signs exam   2

Correct answers for traffic laws and signs exam   6

Traffic laws and signs exam 2   7

Correct answers to traffic laws and signs exam 2   11

Traffic laws and signs exam 3   12

Correct answers for traffic laws and signs exam 3   16

Traffic laws and signs exam 4   17

Correct answers for traffic laws and signs exam 4   21

Traffic laws and signs exam 5   22

Correct answers for traffic laws and signs exam 5   26

Vehicle control and safety   27

This includes knowledge of how to safely operate a vehicle, including the proper use of brakes, steering, and acceleration.

Vehicle control and safety exam   28

Correct answers for vehicle control and safety exam   32

Vehicle control and safety exam 2   33

Correct answers for vehicle control and safety exam 2   37

Vehicle control and safety exam 3   38

Correct answers for vehicle control and safety exam 3   42

Vehicle control and safety exam 4   43

Correct answers for vehicle control and safety exam 4   47

Vehicle control and safety exam 5   48

Correct answers for vehicle control and safety exam 5   52

Alcohol and drugs   53

This includes information about the effects of alcohol and drugs on driving ability, as well as the legal consequences of driving under the influence.

Alcohol and drugs exam 54

Correct answers for alcohol and drugs exam 58

Alcohol and drugs exam 2 59

Correct answers for alcohol and drugs exam 2 62

Alcohol and drugs exam 3 63

Correct answers for alcohol and drugs exam 3 67

Alcohol and drugs exam 4 68

Correct answers for alcohol and drugs exam 4 72

Alcohol and drugs exam 5 73

Correct answers for alcohol and drugs exam 5 77

Vehicle equipment and maintenance 78
This includes knowledge of the various parts of a vehicle and how to properly maintain them, as well as knowledge of how to safely load and unload a vehicle.

Vehicle equipment and maintenance exam 79

Correct answers for vehicle equipment and maintenance exam 83

Vehicle equipment and maintenance exam 2 84

Correct answers for Vehicle equipment and maintenance exam 2 88

Vehicle equipment and maintenance exam 3 89

Correct answers for vehicle equipment and maintenance exam 3 93

Vehicle equipment and maintenance exam 4 94

Correct answers for vehicle equipment and maintenance exam 4 98

Vehicle equipment and maintenance exam 5 100

Correct answers for vehicle equipment and maintenance exam 5 104

Sharing the road 106
This includes information about how to safely share the road with other vehicles, pedestrians, and bicycles.

Sharing the road exam 107

Correct answers for sharing the road exam 111

Sharing the road exam 2 112

Correct answers for sharing the road exam 2 116

Sharing the road exam 3 117

Correct answers for sharing the road exam 3 121

Sharing the road exam 4 122

Correct answers for sharing the road exam 4   126

Sharing the road exam 5   127

Correct answers for sharing the road exam 5   131

Transportation of hazardous materials   132

This includes knowledge of the rules and regulations surrounding the transportation of hazardous materials by commercial vehicles.

Transportation of hazardous materials exam   133

Correct answers for transportation of hazardous materials exam   137

Transportation of hazardous materials exam 2   139

Correct answers for transportation of hazardous materials exam 2   143

Transportation of hazardous materials exam 3   145

Correct answers for transportation of hazardous materials exam 3   149

Transportation of hazardous materials exam 4   150

Correct answers for transportation of hazardous materials exam 4   154

Transportation of hazardous materials exam 5   155

Correct answers for transportation of hazardous materials exam 5   159

Vehicle registration and insurance   160

This includes information about the requirements for registering and insuring a vehicle in Ohio.

Vehicle registration and insurance exam   162

Correct answers for vehicle registration and insurance exam   166

Vehicle registration and insurance exam 2   167

Correct answers for vehicle registration and insurance exam 2   171

Vehicle registration and insurance exam 3   172

Correct answers for vehicle registration and insurance exam 3   176

Vehicle registration and insurance exam 4   177

Correct answers for vehicle registration and insurance exam 4   181

Vehicle registration and insurance exam 5   182

Correct answers for vehicle registration and insurance exam 5   186

Emergencies   187

This includes knowledge of how to handle various types of emergencies that may occur while driving, such as blowouts, fires, and collisions.

Emergencies exam   189

Correct answers for emergencies exam 193

Emergencies exam 2 194

Correct answers for emergencies exam 2 198

Emergencies exam 3 200

Correct answers for emergencies exam 3 204

Emergencies exam 4 205

Correct answers for emergencies exam 4 209

Emergencies exam 5 210

Correct answers for emergencies exam 5 214

Vehicle size and weight limits 215

This includes knowledge of the size and weight limits for vehicles on Ohio roads, as well as the rules for towing.

Vehicle size and weight limits exam 216

Correct answers for vehicle size and weight limits exam 220

Vehicle size and weight limits exam 2 221

Correct answers for vehicle size and weight limits exam 2 225

Vehicle size and weight limits exam 3 226

Correct answers for vehicle size and weight limits exam 3 230

Vehicle size and weight limits exam 4 231

Correct answers for vehicle size and weight limits exam 4 235

Vehicle size and weight limits exam 5 236

Correct answers for vehicle size and weight limits exam 5 240

Public transportation 241

This includes information about the various types of public transportation available in Ohio, as well as the rules for using them.

Public transportation exam 242

Correct answers for public transportation exam 246

Public transportation exam 2 247

Correct answers for public transportation exam 2 251

Public transportation exam 3 252

Correct answers for public transportation exam 3 256

Public transportation exam 4 257

Correct answers for public transportation exam 4   261

Public transportation exam 5   263

Correct answers for public transportation exam 5   267

Conclusion   268

Traffic laws and signs

Driving on the roadways of Ohio requires a deep understanding of traffic laws and signs to ensure the safety of all drivers, passengers, and pedestrians. As a prospective driver, it is important to be familiar with the regulations set forth by the Ohio Department of Motor Vehicles (DMV) to pass the Ohio DMV exam. In this chapter, we will explore the various traffic laws and signs that are essential for all drivers to know.

Traffic laws in Ohio are designed to regulate the flow of vehicles, minimize accidents, and prevent collisions. These laws cover everything from speed limits and right-of-way to signal lights and turn signals. It is important for drivers to be aware of these laws and abide by them at all times while driving on Ohio roads.

Signs are an integral part of the roadways in Ohio and serve as an important means of communicating information to drivers. These signs can be informational, warning or regulatory and are designed to keep drivers informed about the road ahead and help them make informed decisions. From speed limit signs to yield signs, it is important for drivers to know what each sign means and how to react to them.

In this chapter, we will cover the various traffic laws and signs in detail, including the meaning and purpose of each one. We will also go over some common scenarios that drivers may encounter on the roadways and provide tips on how to react in each situation. With the information provided in this chapter, drivers should feel confident and prepared to tackle the Ohio DMV exam.

For training purposes, you can mark the ▢ symbol next to what you think is the correct answer: Once you have chosen the correct answer, use a pencil or pen to mark the ▢ symbol next to that answer.

Traffic laws and signs exam

1. **What does a yellow diamond-shaped sign with a black slash through a bicycle symbol indicate?**

    A. ▢ Bicycles are permitted to ride on the roadway.

    B. ▢ Bicycles are prohibited from riding on the roadway.

    C. ▢ Bicycles are permitted to use the shoulder of the roadway.

    D. ▢ Bicycles are required to dismount and walk.

2. **What does a red octagonal sign mean?**

    A. ▢ Stop

    B. ▢ Yield

    C. ▢ Do not enter

    D. ▢ Slow

3. **What is the speed limit on an Ohio roadway in an urban district when no posted signs are present?**

    A. ▢ 35 mph

    B. ▢ 45 mph

    C. ▢ 25 mph

    D. ▢ 55 mph

4. **What does a blue rectangular sign with a white symbol of a person in a wheelchair indicate?**

    A. ▢ A designated handicap parking space

    B. ▢ A pedestrian crossing

    C. ▢ A sidewalk ramp

D. ▢ A bike lane

5. **What should a driver do when approaching a school bus with flashing red lights?**

A. ▢ Slow down and proceed with caution

B. ▢ Stop, then proceed when the bus starts moving

C. ▢ Increase speed to pass the bus quickly

D. ▢ Stop, regardless of which direction you are driving

6. **What is the speed limit on an Ohio roadway outside of an urban district when no posted signs are present?**

A. ▢ 55 mph

B. ▢ 35 mph

C. ▢ 45 mph

D. ▢ 65 mph

7. **What is the minimum speed a driver can legally travel on Ohio roadways?**

A. ▢ 40 mph

B. ▢ 30 mph

C. ▢ 20 mph

D. ▢ 50 mph

8. **What does a yellow triangle-shaped sign with a black exclamation point indicate?**

A. ▢ Caution

B. ▢ Stop ahead

C. ▢ Yield ahead

D. ▢ Danger ahead

9. **What should a driver do when approaching a yellow flashing traffic signal at an intersection?**

A. ▢ Stop and wait for the signal to turn green

B. ▢ Slow down and proceed with caution

C. ▢ Stop if turning right

D. ▢ Increase speed to beat the red light

10. **What is the minimum distance a driver must stop behind a stopped school bus with flashing red lights?**

A. ▢ 50 feet

B. ▢ 10 feet

C. ▢ 25 feet

D. ▢ 100 feet

11. **What should a driver do when approaching a steady yellow traffic signal at an intersection?**

A. ▢ Stop and wait for the signal to turn green

B. ▢ Slow down and proceed with caution

C. ▢ Increase speed to beat the red light

D. ▢ Stop if turning right

12. **What is the speed limit on Ohio freeways?**

A. ▢ 60 mph

B. ▢ 70 mph

C. ▢ 55 mph

D. ▢ 65 mph

13. What is the minimum following distance a driver must maintain behind the vehicle in front?

A. ▢ 2 seconds

B. ▢ 4 seconds

C. ▢ 1 second

D. ▢ 3 seconds

14. What should a driver do when approaching a red flashing traffic signal at an intersection?

A. ▢ Stop, then proceed when safe

B. ▢ Stop and wait for the signal to turn green

C. ▢ Slow down and proceed with caution

D. ▢ Increase speed to beat the red light

15. What does a white diamond-shaped sign with a black border and black lettering indicate?

A. ▢ A regulatory sign

B. ▢ A warning sign

C. ▢ A guide sign

D. ▢ A service sign

Correct answers for traffic laws and signs exam

1. **B.** Bicycles are prohibited from riding on the roadway.

2. **A.** Stop

3. **C.** 25 mph

4. **A.** A designated handicap parking space

5. **D.** Stop, regardless of which direction you are driving

6. **A.** 55 mph

7. **C.** 20 mph

8. **A.** Caution

9. **B.** Slow down and proceed with caution

10. **A.** 50 feet

11. **B.** Slow down and proceed with caution.

12. **D.** 65 mph

13. **A.** 2 seconds

14. **A.** Stop, then proceed when safe.

15. **A.** A regulatory sign.

Traffic laws and signs exam 2

1. **What is the maximum speed limit in a residential area?**

    A. ▢ 25 mph

    B. ▢ 35 mph

    C. ▢ 20 mph

    D. ▢ 30 mph

2. **What should a driver do when approaching a school crosswalk with a crossing guard present?**

    A. ▢ Slow down and proceed with caution

    B. ▢ Stop and wait for the crossing guard to signal

    C. ▢ Increase speed to cross the crosswalk quickly

    D. ▢ Stop, regardless of whether children are present

3. **What does a yellow square-shaped sign with a black symbol of a truck indicate?**

    A. ▢ A truck route sign

    B. ▢ A no truck sign

    C. ▢ A weight limit sign

    D. ▢ A truck parking sign

4. **What is the maximum speed limit in a business district?**

    A. ▢ 35 mph

    B. ▢ 25 mph

    C. ▢ 30 mph

    D. ▢ 45 mph

5. **What does a white pentagon-shaped sign with a red border and white lettering indicate?**

A. ▢ A stop sign

B. ▢ A yield sign

C. ▢ A do not enter sign

D. ▢ A warning sign

6. **What is the maximum speed limit on a residential street?**

A. ▢ 35 mph

B. ▢ 40 mph

C. ▢ 45 mph

D. ▢ 30 mph

7. **What does a yellow diamond-shaped sign indicate?**

A. ▢ Stop

B. ▢ Yield

C. ▢ Pedestrian Crossing

D. ▢ No parking

8. **What does a red octagon shape sign indicate?**

A. ▢ Stop

B. ▢ Yield

C. ▢ Pedestrian Crossing

D. ▢ No parking

9. What is the minimum speed limit on a highway?

A. ▢ 45 mph

B. ▢ 50 mph

C. ▢ 55 mph

D. ▢ 60 mph

10. What is the penalty for driving under the influence of alcohol?

A. ▢ Fine

B. ▢ License Suspension

C. ▢ Imprisonment

D. ▢ All of the above

11. When should you use your turn signals?

A. ▢ Only when changing lanes

B. ▢ Only when turning

C. ▢ Whenever you change direction or speed on the road

D. ▢ Never

12. What is the proper action to take when approaching a school bus with its red lights flashing?

A. ▢ Pass the bus

B. ▢ Slow down and be prepared to stop

C. ◻ Speed up to get past the bus

D. ◻ Drive on as normal

13. What does a blue rectangular sign with a white border indicate?

A. ◻ Stop

B. ◻ Information

C. ◻ Warning

D. ◻ Speed limit

14. What is the fine for texting while driving?

A. ◻ $50

B. ◻ $100

C. ◻ $150

D. ◻ $200

15. What is the minimum age to obtain a driver's license in most states?

A. ◻ 16 years old

B. ◻ 17 years old

C. ◻ 18 years old

D. ◻ 19 years old

Correct answers to traffic laws and signs exam 2

1. **A.** 25 mph
2. **B.** Stop and wait for the crossing guard to signal.
3. **A.** A truck route sign.
4. **B.** 25 mph.
5. **A.** A stop sign.
6. **D.** 30 mph
7. **B.** Yield
8. **A.** Stop
9. **C.** 55 mph
10. **D.** All of the above
11. **C.** Whenever you change direction or speed on the road
12. **B.** Slow down and be prepared to stop
13. **B.** Information
14. **C.** $150
15. **A.** 16 years old

Traffic laws and signs exam 3

1. **What does a yellow traffic light mean?**

A. □ Stop immediately

B. □ Slow down and proceed with caution

C. □ Speed up to beat the light

D. □ Drive through without slowing down

2. **What does a red and white "STOP" sign indicate?**

A. □ Yield to other vehicles

B. □ Stop and wait for further instructions

C. □ Stop before proceeding

D. □ Keep moving, no need to stop

3. **What is the maximum speed limit in a school zone?**

A. □ 35 mph

B. □ 40 mph

C. □ 45 mph

D. □ 25 mph

4. **What does a "Do Not Enter" sign indicate?**

A. □ One way road ahead

B. □ U-turn allowed

C. □ Road ahead is closed

D. □ Drive in the opposite direction

5. **What does a "Yield" sign indicate?**

A. ▫ Stop before proceeding

B. ▫ Give the right of way to other vehicles

C. ▫ Make a U-turn

D. ▫ Speed up to beat other vehicles

6. **What is the minimum speed limit on the highway?**

A. ▫ 45 mph

B. ▫ 50 mph

C. ▫ 60 mph

D. ▫ There is no minimum speed limit

7. **What does a "No Parking" sign indicate?**

A. ▫ Parking allowed anytime

B. ▫ Parking allowed during certain hours

C. ▫ No parking at any time

D. ▫ Parking allowed for a limited time

8. **What does a "Speed Limit" sign indicate?**

A. ▫ Recommended speed

B. ▫ Maximum speed limit

C. ▫ Minimum speed limit

D. ▫ Average speed limit

9. **What does a "No U-Turn" sign indicate?**

A. ▫ U-turn allowed

B. ▫ U-turn not allowed

C. ▫ U-turn allowed during certain hours

D. ▢ Make a U-turn at your own risk

10. What does a "No Passing" sign indicate?

A. ▢ Passing allowed at all times

B. ▢ Passing allowed during certain hour

C. ▢ No passing except on the left

D. ▢ No passing except on the right

11. What does a green traffic light mean?

A. ▢ Stop before proceeding

B. ▢ Slow down and proceed with caution

C. ▢ Drive through without slowing down

D. ▢ Go ahead

12. What does a "Pedestrian Crossing" sign indicate?

A. ▢ Pedestrians not allowed

B. ▢ Look out for pedestrians

C. ▢ Pedestrians have the right of way

D. ▢ Pedestrians are prohibited

13. What is the maximum speed limit in a residential area?

A. ▢ 35 mph

B. ▢ 40 mph

C. ▢ 45 mph

D. ▢ 25 mph

14. What does a green traffic light mean?

A. ▢ Driving in the wrong direction

B. ▢ Turn around

C. ▢ Do not enter

D. ▢ Drive ahead

15. What does a "Yield to Pedestrians" sign indicate?

A. ▢ Stop before proceeding

B. ▢ Give the right of way to pedestrians

C. ▢ Make a U-turn

D. ▢ Speed up to beat other vehicles

Correct answers for traffic laws and signs exam 3

1. **B. Sl**ow down and proceed with caution
2. **C.** Stop before proceeding
3. **D.** 25 mph
4. **A.** One way road ahead
5. **B.** Give the right of way to other vehicles
6. **D. T**here is no minimum speed limit
7. **C.** No parking at any time
8. **B.** Maximum speed limit
9. **B.** U-turn not allowed
10. **C.** No passing except on the left
11. **D.** Go ahead
12. **C.** Pedestrians have the right of way
13. **D.** 25 mph
14. **C.** Do not enter
15. **B.** Give the right of way to pedestrians

Traffic laws and signs exam 4

1. **What is the minimum speed limit on a two-lane road?**

   A. ▫ 45 mph

   B. ▫ 50 mph

   C. ▫ 60 mph

   D. ▫ There is no minimum speed limit

2. **What does a "No Stopping" sign indicate?**

   A. ▫ Stopping allowed anytime

   B. ▫ Stopping allowed during certain hours

   C. ▫ No stopping at any time

   D. ▫ Stopping allowed for a limited time

3. **What does a "Speed Limit Ends" sign indicate?**

   A. ▫ Recommended speed

   B. ▫ Maximum speed limit

   C. ▫ The end of a speed limit zone

   D. ▫ Minimum speed limit

4. **What does a "No Left Turn" sign indicate?**

   A. ▫ Left turn allowed

   B. ▫ Left turn not allowed

   C. ▫ Left turn allowed during certain hours

   D. ▫ Make a left turn at your own risk

5. **What does a "Keep Right" sign indicate?**

A. ▢ Drive on the left side

B. ▢ Keep to the right side of the road

C. ▢ Drive on the right side

D. ▢ Keep to the left side of the road

6. **What does a red traffic light mean?**

A. ▢ Stop

B. ▢ Go

C. ▢ Slow down

D. ▢ Yield

7. **What is the speed limit in a school zone during school hours?**

A. ▢ 25 mph

B. ▢ 30 mph

C. ▢ 35 mph

D. ▢ 40 mph

8. **What does a yellow triangle road sign indicate?**

A. ▢ Stop ahead

B. ▢ Yield ahead

C. ▢ Pedestrian crossing

D. ▢ School zone

9. **When should you use your turn signals?**

A. ▢ When changing lanes

B. ▢ When making a turn

C. ▫ When driving in a straight line

D. ▫ Only in the rain

10. What does a green arrow on a traffic signal mean?

A. ▫ Go

B. ▫ Stop

C. ▫ Slow down

D. ▫ Yield

11. What does a solid white line on the road indicate?

A. ▫ Separation between lanes of traffic moving in the same direction

B. ▫ Divider between opposing lanes of traffic

C. ▫ Bicycle lane

D. ▫ No passing zone

12. What should you do when approaching a stopped school bus with flashing red lights?

A. ▫ Slow down and proceed with caution

B. ▫ Stop

C. ▫ Speed up to pass the bus

D. ▫ Keep driving without slowing down

13. What should you do when driving in heavy rain?

A. ▫ Increase your speed to get to your destination faster

B. ▫ Drive in the center lane

C. ▫ Slow down and maintain a safe following distance

D. ▫ Drive as you normally do

14. What does a sign with an image of a red octagon mean?

A. ▢ Stop

B. ▢ Yield

C. ▢ Go

D. ▢ Slow down

15. What does a sign with an image of a pedestrian and the words "walk" mean?

A. ▢ Pedestrian crossing

B. ▢ School zone

C. ▢ Stop

D. ▢ Yield

Correct answers for traffic laws and signs exam 4

1. **D.** There is no minimum speed limit
2. **C.** No stopping at any time
3. **C.** The end of a speed limit zone
4. **B.** Left turn not allowed
5. **B.** Keep to the right side of the road
6. **A.** Stop
7. **B.** 30 mph
8. **B.** Yield ahead
9. **B.** When making a turn
10. **A.** Go
11. **A.** Separation between lanes of traffic moving in the same direction
12. **B.** Stop
13. **C.** Slow down and maintain a safe following distance
14. **A.** Stop
15. **A.** Pedestrian crossing

Traffic laws and signs exam 5

1. **What does a "Do Not Enter" sign mean?**

A. ▢ One way street

B. ▢ Stop

C. ▢ Yield

D. ▢ Enter

2. **What does a flashing yellow light mean?**

A. ▢ Stop

B. ▢ Yield

C. ▢ Proceed with caution

D. ▢ Go

3. **What is the speed limit in a residential area?**

A. ▢ 25 mph

B. ▢ 30 mph

C. ▢ 35 mph

D. ▢ 40 mph

4. **When should you use your high beams?**

A. ▢ When driving on a bright sunny day

B. ▢ When driving in heavy rain

C. ▢ When there is no oncoming traffic

D. ▢ When passing another vehicle

5. **What does a sign with an image of a deer mean?**

A. ▢ Wildlife crossing

B. ▢ No parking

C. ▢ No passing zone

D. ▢ Stop

6. **What should you do when you see a yield sign?**

A. ▢ Stop

B. ▢ Go

C. ▢ Yield to other vehicles on the road

D. ▢ Proceed with caution

7. **What does a sign with an image of a bicycle and the words "bike lane" mean?**

A. ▢ Bicycle lane

B. ▢ Pedestrian crossing

C. ▢ School zone

D. ▢ No parking

8. **What should you do when you approach a railroad crossing with no gates or signals?**

A. ▢ Stop and proceed with caution

B. ▢ Speed up to get across the tracks quickly

C. ▢ Slow down and be prepared to stop if a train is coming

D. ▢ Keep driving without slowing down

9. **What is the minimum following distance you should maintain behind the vehicle in front of you?**

A. ▢ 2 seconds

B. ▢ 3 seconds

C. ▫ 4 seconds

D. ▫ 5 seconds

10. What does a sign with an image of a wheelchair and the words "handicap parking" mean?

A. ▫ Handicap parking

B. ▫ No parking

C. ▫ No stopping

D. ▫ School zone

11. What should you do when driving on a road with a solid yellow line on your side?

A. ▫ Pass other vehicles

B. ▫ Follow closely behind other vehicles

C. ▫ Drive in the center lane

D. ▫ Do not cross the yellow line

12. What does a sign with an image of a truck and the words "truck route" mean?

A. ▫ Truck route

B. ▫ Pedestrian crossing

C. ▫ No parking

D. ▫ Stop

13. What is the speed limit on an expressway with no posted speed limit signs?

A. ▫ 25 mph

B. ▫ 30 mph

C. ▫ 55 mph

D. ▫ 65 mph

14. When should you use your hazard lights?

A. ▢ When driving in fog

B. ▢ When driving in heavy rain

C. ▢ When your vehicle has broken down on the side of the road

D. ▢ When you want to warn other drivers of a dangerous situation

15. What does a sign with an image of a diamond shape mean?

A. ▢ Pedestrian crossing

B. ▢ Yield

C. ▢ Stop

D. ▢ Warning

Correct answers for traffic laws and signs exam 5

1. **A.** One way street

2. **C.** Proceed with caution

3. **A.** 25 mph

4. **C.** When there is no oncoming traffic

5. **A.** Wildlife crossing

6. **C.** Yield to other vehicles on the road

7. **A.** Bicycle lane

8. **C.** Slow down and be prepared to stop if a train is coming

9. **A.** 2 seconds

10. **A.** Handicap parking

11. **D.** Do not cross the yellow line

12. **A.** Truck route

13. **D.** 65 mph

14. **C.** When your vehicle has broken down on the side of the road

15. **D.** Warning

Vehicle control and safety

Driving is a privilege that comes with great responsibility. One of the most important aspects of operating a vehicle is maintaining control and ensuring safety for both yourself and others on the road. The Ohio Department of Motor Vehicles (DMV) requires that all aspiring drivers demonstrate their understanding of these concepts in order to receive a driver's license. In this chapter, we will cover the fundamentals of vehicle control and safety as they relate to the Ohio DMV exam.

Vehicle control involves the ability to maneuver your vehicle in a safe and controlled manner. This includes understanding how to steer, accelerate, and brake effectively, as well as maintaining stability on the road, even in adverse weather conditions. It's also important to understand the different types of roadways and how to adjust your driving to the specific conditions of each.

Safety is a crucial component of driving, and there are several key practices that you should be aware of in order to keep yourself and others safe on the road. These include wearing seat belts, following the speed limit, avoiding distractions, and always being aware of other drivers and their actions. In addition, you should be familiar with the laws and regulations that govern driving in Ohio, as well as the consequences for violating these laws.

In the Ohio DMV exam, you will be tested on your knowledge of vehicle control and safety, and it's essential that you have a thorough understanding of these concepts in order to pass the exam and become a licensed driver. This chapter will provide you with the information you need to succeed on the exam and become a safe and responsible driver on the road.

For training purposes, you can mark the ▢ symbol next to what you think is the correct answer: Once you have chosen the correct answer, use a pencil or pen to mark the ▢ symbol next to that answer.

Vehicle control and safety exam

1. **What is the appropriate following distance when driving behind another vehicle?**

    A. ▫ One car length for every 10 mph of speed

    B. ▫ Two car lengths for every 10 mph of speed

    C. ▫ Three car lengths for every 10 mph of speed

    D. ▫ Four car lengths for every 10 mph of speed

2. **What should you do if your brakes fail while driving?**

    A. ▫ Pump the brakes repeatedly

    B. ▫ Downshift to a lower gear

    C. ▫ Use the emergency brake

    D. ▫ Steer the car to the side of the road

3. **What should you do when approaching a yellow light at an intersection?**

    A. ▫ Speed up to make it through the intersection

    B. ▫ Stop if it is safe to do so

    C. ▫ Accelerate to beat the red light

    D. ▫ Maintain the same speed

4. **What is the minimum age to obtain a driver's license in Ohio?**

    A. ▫ 15 years old

    B. ▫ 16 years old

    C. ▫ 17 years old

    D. ▫ 18 years old

5. **What should you do when merging onto a highway?**

A. ▢ Slow down and let other vehicles merge in front of you

B. ▢ Speed up and merge into the flow of traffic

C. ▢ Stop at the end of the ramp and wait for an opening

D. ▢ Honk your horn to signal other drivers to let you in

6. **When driving in inclement weather, what is the best way to maintain control of your vehicle?**

A. ▢ Drive as fast as possible

B. ▢ Use cruise control

C. ▢ Decrease your speed and maintain a safe following distance

D. ▢ Ignore the weather and drive as usual

7. **What should you do if you are being tailgated by another driver?**

A. ▢ Speed up to get away from the tailgater

B. ▢ Brake suddenly to teach the tailgater a lesson

C. ▢ Move to another lane if possible and let the tailgater pass

D. ▢ Honk your horn and make gestures at the tailgater

8. **What is the maximum speed limit in Ohio for vehicles traveling on rural interstates?**

A. ▢ 60 mph

B. ▢ 65 mph

C. ▢ 70 mph

D. ▢ 75 mph

9. **What should you do if you approach a railroad crossing and the crossing gates are down?**

A. ▢ Stop before the crossing and wait for the gates to rise

B. ▢ Drive around the gates

C. ☐ Drive through the crossing as quickly as possible

D. ☐ Honk your horn to signal the train to move

10. What should you do when approaching a roundabout?

A. ☐ Slow down and yield to vehicles already in the roundabout

B. ☐ Stop and wait for all vehicles to clear the roundabout

C. ☐ Drive around the roundabout in a counterclockwise direction

D. ☐ Cut off other vehicles to enter the roundabout first

11. What should you do when approaching a blind intersection?

A. ☐ Slow down and proceed with caution

B. ☐ Speed up and cross the intersection quickly

C. ☐ Honk your horn to warn other drivers

D. ☐ Stop and wait for other drivers to cross first

12. What is the minimum amount of liability insurance required by law in Ohio?

A. ☐ $10,000

B. ☐ $25,000

C. ☐ $50,000

D. ☐ $100,000

13. What should you do when approaching a stopped school bus with flashing red lights?

A. ☐ Continue driving at the same speed

B. ☐ Slow down and proceed with caution

C. ☐ Stop and wait for the bus to resume motion

D. ☐ Drive around the bus on the left side

14. What should you do if you are driving on a slippery road and begin to skid?

A. ▢ Apply the brakes

B. ▢ Steer in the direction of the skid

C. ▢ Accelerate to regain traction

D. ▢ Turn off the road and park

15. What is the legal blood alcohol concentration limit in Ohio for drivers over the age of 21?

A. ▢ 0.05%

B. ▢ 0.08%

C. ▢ 0.10%

D. ▢ 0.15%

Correct answers for vehicle control and safety exam

1. **C.** Three car lengths for every 10 mph of speed

2. **C.** Use the emergency brake

3. **B.** Stop if it is safe to do so

4. **B.** 16 years old

5. **B.** Speed up and merge into the flow of traffic

6. **C.** Decrease your speed and maintain a safe following distance

7. **C.** Move to another lane if possible and let the tailgater pass

8. **C.** 70 mph

9. **A.** Stop before the crossing and wait for the gates to rise

10. **A.** Slow down and yield to vehicles already in the roundabout

11. **A.** Slow down and proceed with caution

12. **B.** $25,000

13. **C.** Stop and wait for the bus to resume motion

14. **B.** Steer in the direction of the skid

15. **B.** 0.08%

Vehicle control and safety exam 2

1. **What is the purpose of the accelerator pedal in a vehicle?**

   A. ▢ To control the speed of the vehicle

   B. ▢ To control the direction of the vehicle

   C. ▢ To control the volume of the radio

   D. ▢ To control the headlights of the vehicle

2. **What is the primary function of the brake pedal in a vehicle?**

   A. ▢ To increase the speed of the vehicle

   B. ▢ To control the direction of the vehicle

   C. ▢ To stop the vehicle

   D. ▢ To control the volume of the radio

3. **What is the purpose of the steering wheel in a vehicle?**

   A. ▢ To control the volume of the radio

   B. ▢ To control the speed of the vehicle

   C. ▢ To control the direction of the vehicle

   D. ▢ To control the headlights of the vehicle

4. **What is the purpose of the seat belt in a vehicle?**

   A. ▢ To control the speed of the vehicle

   B. ▢ To control the direction of the vehicle

   C. ▢ To provide comfort for the passengers

   D. ▢ To protect the passengers in case of an accident

5. **What is the purpose of the headlights in a vehicle?**

A. ▢ To provide light for the driver to see the road ahead

B. ▢ To control the speed of the vehicle

C. ▢ To control the direction of the vehicle

D. ▢ To control the volume of the radio

6. **What is the purpose of the turn signals in a vehicle?**

A. ▢ To indicate to other drivers the intention to turn or change lanes

B. ▢ To control the speed of the vehicle

C. ▢ To control the direction of the vehicl

D. ▢ To control the volume of the radio

7. **What is the purpose of the backup camera in a vehicle?**

A. ▢ To provide a view behind the vehicle when reversing

B. ▢ To control the speed of the vehicle

C. ▢ To control the direction of the vehicle

D. ▢ To control the volume of the radio

8. **What is the purpose of the anti-lock braking system (ABS) in a vehicle?**

A. ▢ To prevent the wheels from locking up and skidding during hard braking

B. ▢ To control the speed of the vehicle

C. ▢ To control the direction of the vehicle

D. ▢ To control the volume of the radio

9. **What is the purpose of the stability control system in a vehicle?**

A. ▢ To improve the stability and handling of the vehicle during sudden maneuvers

B. ▢ To control the speed of the vehicle

C. ▢ To control the direction of the vehicle

D. ▢ To control the volume of the radio

10. What is the purpose of the airbags in a vehicle?

A. ▢ To provide cushioning in case of an accident to protect the passengers

B. ▢ To control the speed of the vehicle

C. ▢ To control the direction of the vehicle

D. ▢ To control the volume of the radio

11. What is the primary function of the accelerator pedal in a vehicle?

A. ▢ To control the speed of the vehicle

B. ▢ To control the direction of the vehicle

C. ▢ To control the volume of the radio

D. ▢ To control the windshield wipers of the vehicle

12. What is the purpose of the brake pedal in a vehicle?

A. ▢ To increase the speed of the vehicle

B. ▢ To control the direction of the vehicle

C. ▢ To stop the vehicle

D. ▢ To control the radio volume

13. What is the function of the steering wheel in a vehicle?

A. ▢ To control the volume of the radio

B. ▢ To control the speed of the ve

C. ▢ To control the direction of the vehicle

D. ▢ To control the windshield wipers of the vehicle

14. What should you do if you approach a vehicle with flashing hazard lights on the side of the road?

A. ▢ Slow down and be prepared to stop

B. ▢ Speed up and pass quickly

C. ▢ Change lanes

D. ▢ Maintain your speed

15. What is the main function of the headlights in a vehicle?

A. ▢ To provide light for the driver to see the road ahead

B. ▢ To control the speed of the vehicle

C. ▢ To control the direction of the vehicle

D. ▢ To control the windshield wipers of the vehicle

Correct answers for vehicle control and safety exam 2

1. **A.** To control the speed of the vehicle
2. **C.** To stop the vehicle
3. **C.** To control the direction of the vehicle
4. **D.** To protect the passengers in case of an accident
5. **A.** To provide light for the driver to see the road ahead
6. **A.** To indicate to other drivers the intention to turn or change lanes
7. **A.** To provide a view behind the vehicle when reversing
8. **A.** To prevent the wheels from locking up and skidding during hard braking
9. **A.** To improve the stability and handling of the vehicle during sudden maneuvers
10. **A.** To provide cushioning in case of an accident to protect the passengers
11. **A.** To control the speed of the vehicle
12. **C.** To stop the vehicle
13. **C.** To control the direction of the vehicle
14. **A.** Slow down and be prepared to stop
15. **A.** To provide light for the driver to see the road ahead

Vehicle control and safety exam 3

1. **What is the purpose of a seatbelt in a vehicle?**

   A. ▢ To increase passenger comfort

   B. ▢ To provide a convenient place to hang shopping bags

   C. ▢ To increase the weight of the vehicle

   D. ▢ To increase passenger safety

2. **What should you do when you experience a blowout while driving?**

   A. ▢ Slam on the brakes

   B. ▢ Steer in the direction of the blowout

   C. ▢ Gradually reduce speed and safely pull off the road

   D. ▢ Accelerate to maintain control of the vehicle

3. **What is the appropriate action to take when approaching a stop sign?**

   A. ▢ Stop only if there are other vehicles present

   B. ▢ Slow down and proceed with caution

   C. ▢ Stop completely before the crosswalk

   D. ▢ Slow down and proceed without stopping

4. **What is the main function of anti-lock brakes in a vehicle?**

   A. ▢ To provide better control in slippery conditions

   B. ▢ To shorten the stopping distance

   C. ▢ To make the brakes more durable

   D. ▢ To make the vehicle faster

5. **What should you do if your vehicle starts to hydroplane on a wet road?**

A. ▢ Accelerate to regain traction

B. ▢ Brake firmly

C. ▢ Steer in the direction you want the vehicle to go

D. ▢ None of the above

6. **What is the recommended speed limit in a school zone?**

A. ▢ 25 mph

B. ▢ 30 mph

C. ▢ 35 mph

D. ▢ 40 mph

7. **What is the appropriate action to take when encountering a yellow light at an intersection?**

A. ▢ Speed up to get through the intersection

B. ▢ Stop if it is safe to do so

C. ▢ Proceed with caution

D. ▢ None of the above

8. **What is the recommended minimum following distance when driving in good weather conditions?**

A. ▢ 2 seconds

B. ▢ 3 seconds

C. ▢ 4 seconds

D. ▢ 5 seconds

9. **What should you do if your vehicle begins to skid on a slippery road?**

A. ▢ Apply the brakes

B. ▢ Turn the steering wheel in the direction of the skid

C. ▫ Accelerate to regain traction

D. ▫ None of the above

10. What is the purpose of a blind spot mirror in a vehicle?

A. ▫ To reduce the size of the blind spot

B. ▫ To eliminate the blind spot completely

C. ▫ To increase the size of the blind spot

D. ▫ None of the above

11. What is the recommended minimum following distance when driving behind a vehicle in rainy weather?

A. ▫ 3 seconds

B. ▫ 4 seconds

C. ▫ 5 seconds

D. ▫ 6 seconds

12. What should you do when approaching a pedestrian crossing?

A. ▫ Slow down and proceed with caution

B. ▫ Honk the horn to warn the pedestrian

C. ▫ Stop completely and wait for the pedestrian to cross

D. ▫ Speed up to get past the crossing quickly

13. What is the appropriate speed limit in a residential area?

A. ▫ 25 mph

B. ▫ 30 mph

C. ▫ 35 mph

D. ▫ 40 mph

14. What should you do when changing lanes on a multi-lane road?

A. ▢ Signal your intention to change lanes

B. ▢ Check your blind spot

C. ▢ Both a and b

D. ▢ None of the above

15. What is the recommended minimum following distance when driving behind a large truck?

A. ▢ 4 seconds

B. ▢ 5 seconds

C. ▢ 6 seconds

D. ▢ 7 seconds

Correct answers for vehicle control and safety exam 3

1. **D.** To increase passenger safety

2. **C.** Gradually reduce speed and safely pull off the road

3. **C.** Stop completely before the crosswalk

4. **A.** To provide better control in slippery conditions

5. **C.** Steer in the direction you want the vehicle to go

6. **A.** 25 mph

7. **B.** Stop if it is safe to do so

8. **B.** 3 seconds

9. **B.** Turn the steering wheel in the direction of the skid

10. **A.** To reduce the size of the blind spot

11. **D.** 6 seconds

12. **C.** Stop completely and wait for the pedestrian to cross

13. **A.** 25 mph

14. **C.** Both a and b

15. **D.** 7 seconds

Vehicle control and safety exam 4

1. **What is the recommended action to take when approaching a red light at an intersection?**

A. ▢ Stop before entering the crosswalk

B. ▢ Slow down and proceed with caution

C. ▢ Stop only if there are other vehicles present

D. ▢ Run the red light if no one is around

2. **What is the recommended speed limit on an expressway with no posted speed limit signs?**

A. ▢ 50 mph

B. ▢ 55 mph

C. ▢ 60 mph

D. ▢ 65 mph

3. **What is the recommended action to take when your vehicle begins to skid on a slippery road?**

A. ▢ Steer in the direction you want the vehicle to go

B. ▢ Apply the brakes

C. ▢ Accelerate to regain traction

D. ▢ None of the above

4. **What is the purpose of a crumple zone in a vehicle?**

A. ▢ To provide a comfortable place for passengers to rest their feet

B. ▢ To absorb impact energy in the event of a collision

C. ▢ To make the vehicle more aerodynamic

D. ▢ To reduce the weight of the vehicle

5. **What is the recommended action to take when encountering a deer on the road while driving?**

A. ◻ Brake firmly

B. ◻ Swerve to avoid the deer

C. ◻ Slow down and proceed with caution

D. ◻ Honk the horn to scare the deer away

6. **What is the main purpose of a seat belt in a vehicle?**

A. ◻ To keep the driver comfortable

B. ◻ To secure loose items

C. ◻ To prevent injury during an accident

D. ◻ To control the speed of the vehicle

7. **What is the recommended tire pressure for a vehicle?**

A. ◻ 20 PSI

B. ◻ 30 PSI

C. ◻ 40 PSI

D. ◻ 50 PSI

8. **What is ABS in a vehicle?**

A. ◻ Anti-lock Brake System

B. ◻ Automatic Brake System

C. ◻ Active Brake System

D. ◻ Advanced Brake System

9. **What is the purpose of a catalytic converter in a vehicle?**

A. ◻ To control the speed of the vehicle

B. ◻ To reduce emissions from the engine

C. ☐ To improve fuel efficiency

D. ☐ To regulate air conditioning

10. What is the minimum distance to maintain between two vehicles while driving?

A. ☐ 3 feet

B. ☐ 5 feet

C. ☐ 7 feet

D. ☐ 10 feet

11. What should you do if you are involved in a car accident?

A. ☐ Leave the scene of the accident

B. ☐ Exchange insurance information with the other driver

C. ☐ Call the police

D. ☐ All of the above

12. What is the recommended frequency for checking the oil level in a vehicle?

A. ☐ Once a week

B. ☐ Twice a month

C. ☐ Once a month

D. ☐ Twice a week

13. What is the purpose of a horn in a vehicle?

A. ☐ To alert other drivers

B. ☐ To signal the driver's presence

C. ☐ To communicate with passengers

D. ☐ To play music

14. What is the speed limit in a school zone during school hours?

A. ▢ 25 mph

B. ▢ 30 mph

C. ▢ 35 mph

D. ▢ 40 mph

15. What is the recommended practice for using a turn signal while driving?

A. ▢ Only use it occasionally

B. ▢ Use it only when necessary

C. ▢ Use it frequently to indicate intent

D. ▢ Never use it

Correct answers for vehicle control and safety exam 4

1. **A.** Stop before entering the crosswalk

2. **D.** 65 mph

3. **A.** Steer in the direction you want the vehicle to go

4. **B.** To absorb impact energy in the event of a collision

5. **B.** Swerve to avoid the deer

6. **C.** To prevent injury during an accident

7. **B.** 30 PSI

8. **A.** Anti-lock Brake System

9. **B.** To reduce emissions from the engine

10. **B.** 5 feet

11. **C.** Call the police

12. **C.** Once a month

13. **A.** To alert other drivers

14. **A.** 25 mph

15. **C.** Use it frequently to indicate intent

Vehicle control and safety exam 5

1. **What is the main function of the car's braking system?**

   A. ▢ To control speed

   B. ▢ To provide power to the engine

   C. ▢ To stop the vehicle

   D. ▢ To steer the vehicle

2. **What is the purpose of the seat belts in a vehicle?**

   A. ▢ To provide comfort while driving

   B. ▢ To improve the car's appearance

   C. ▢ To keep the driver and passengers in place during sudden stops or collisions

   D. ▢ To control air flow in the car

3. **What type of airbags are required in all vehicles by federal law?**

   A. ▢ Side airbags

   B. ▢ Front airbags

   C. ▢ Rear airbags

   D. ▢ Knee airbags

4. **What is the recommended tire pressure for a vehicle?**

   A. ▢ The pressure listed on the tire sidewall

   B. ▢ The pressure listed in the vehicle owner's manual

   C. ▢ The highest pressure possible

   D. ▢ The lowest pressure possible

5. **What is the purpose of Anti-Lock Braking System (ABS) in a vehicle?**

A. ▢ To improve fuel efficiency

B. ▢ To provide better grip on slippery roads

C. ▢ To reduce stopping distance

D. ▢ To increase top speed

6. **What should you do if your vehicle begins to skid on a wet road?**

A. ▢ Steer in the direction of the skid

B. ▢ Steer in the opposite direction of the skid

C. ▢ Brake firmly

D. ▢ Accelerate

7. **What is the minimum legal tread depth for a tire in the United States?**

A. ▢ 2/32 inch

B. ▢ 4/32 inch

C. ▢ 6/32 inch

D. ▢ 8/32 inch

8. **What is the correct way to check tire pressure?**

A. ▢ When the tire is cold

B. ▢ When the tire is hot

C. ▢ When the tire is inflating

D. ▢ When the tire is deflating

9. **What should you do if your vehicle experiences a blowout while driving?**

A. ▢ Apply the brakes firmly

B. ▢ Accelerate

C. ▢ Steer in the direction of the blowout

D. ▫ Gradually reduce speed and pull off the road

10. What is the recommended following distance between vehicles on the highway?

A. ▫ 3 seconds

B. ▫ 4 seconds

C. ▫ 5 seconds

D. ▫ 6 seconds

11. What is the purpose of a car's exhaust system?

A. ▫ To reduce engine noise

B. ▫ To improve engine performance

C. ▫ To remove harmful gases from the engine

D. ▫ To regulate engine temperature

12. What type of ignition system is commonly found in most vehicles?

A. ▫ Distributor-based ignition system

B. ▫ Electronic ignition system

C. ▫ Hybrid ignition system

D. ▫ Mechanical ignition system

13. What is the purpose of a car's electrical system?

A. ▫ To deliver electrical power to various components in the vehicle

B. ▫ To provide lighting for the vehicle

C. ▫ To start the engine

D. ▫ All of the above

14. What type of fuel is commonly used in most vehicles?

A. ▢ Diesel fuel

B. ▢ Gasoline

C. ▢ Propane

D. ▢ Electric power

15. What is the purpose of a car's battery?

A. ▢ To provide electrical power to start the engine

B. ▢ To provide electrical power to run the vehicle's lights and electronics

C. ▢ To recharge the car's alternator

D. ▢ All of the above

Correct answers for vehicle control and safety exam 5

1. **C.** To stop the vehicle
2. **C.** To keep the driver and passengers in place during sudden stops or collisions
3. **B.** Front airbags
4. **B.** The pressure listed in the vehicle owner's manual
5. **B.** To provide better grip on slippery roads
6. **B.** Steer in the opposite direction of the skid
7. **A.** 2/32 inch
8. **A.** When the tire is cold
9. **D.** Gradually reduce speed and pull off the road
10. **C.** 5 seconds
11. **C.** To remove harmful gases from the engine
12. **B.** Electronic ignition system
13. **D.** All of the above
14. **B.** Gasoline
15. **D.** All of the above

Alcohol and drugs

Alcohol and drug use are major contributors to traffic accidents and fatalities on the roads. In an effort to keep drivers safe, Ohio DMV has included questions about the effects of alcohol and drugs on driving as part of its licensing exam. It's important for aspiring drivers to understand the dangers of operating a vehicle while under the influence of these substances and the laws surrounding them.

In Ohio, the legal blood alcohol concentration (BAC) limit for drivers over the age of 21 is .08%. However, even small amounts of alcohol can impair a driver's abilities, including reaction time, judgement, and coordination. Additionally, it's against the law to operate a vehicle under the influence of drugs, regardless of whether they are prescription, over-the-counter, or illegal.

It's important to note that the effects of alcohol and drugs can vary depending on the individual, the amount consumed, and the type of substance. In some cases, the effects can last long after the individual has stopped feeling drunk or high. This can pose a serious danger to other drivers, passengers, and pedestrians on the road.

In Ohio, a conviction for driving under the influence (DUI) can result in significant fines, jail time, and the loss of driving privileges. The severity of the punishment depends on the circumstances of the offense, such as the BAC level at the time of the arrest and any prior convictions for DUI.

As aspiring drivers prepare for the Ohio DMV licensing exam, it's crucial for them to have a solid understanding of the dangers of driving under the influence of alcohol and drugs and the laws surrounding them. The questions on the exam will test their knowledge on these topics and their commitment to driving safely and responsibly.

In this chapter, we will take a closer look at the effects of alcohol and drugs on driving, the laws and consequences surrounding DUI in Ohio, and the type of questions to expect on the Ohio DMV licensing exam related to these topics. By the end of this chapter, aspiring drivers will have a comprehensive understanding of the importance of safe and responsible driving and how to avoid the dangers of operating a vehicle under the influence of alcohol and drugs.

For training purposes, you can mark the ▢ symbol next to what you think is the correct answer: Once you have chosen the correct answer, use a pencil or pen to mark the ▢ symbol next to that answer.

Alcohol and drugs exam

1. **What is the legal blood alcohol concentration (BAC) limit for drivers over the age of 21 in Ohio?**

   A. ▢ 0.05%

   B. ▢ 0.08%

   C. ▢ 0.10%

   D. ▢ 0.12%

2. **What is the penalty for a first-time DUI conviction in Ohio?**

   A. ▢ $500 fine and 90-day license suspension

   B. ▢ $1,000 fine and 1-year license suspension

   C. ▢ $2,500 fine and 2-year license suspension

   D. ▢ $5,000 fine and 3-year license suspension

3. **Which of the following is not an effect of alcohol on driving?**

   A. ▢ Impairment of judgement

   B. ▢ Increased reaction time

   C. ▢ Decreased coordination

   D. ▢ Increased focus

4. **Can you be arrested for DUI in Ohio if you are under the influence of prescription drugs?**

   A. ▢ Yes

   B. ▢ No

   C. ▢ Only if the prescription drug is not legally obtained

   D. ▢ Only if the prescription drug impairs your driving abilities

5. **What is the maximum fine for a third DUI conviction in Ohio?**

A. ▢ $1,000

B. ▢ $2,500

C. ▢ $10,000

D. ▢ $15,000

6. **Which of the following is not an effect of drugs on driving?**

A. ▢ Decreased reaction time

B. ▢ Impaired judgement

C. ▢ Increased focus

D. ▢ Decreased coordination

7. **How long does a DUI conviction stay on your driving record in Ohio?**

A. ▢ 1 year

B. ▢ 3 years

C. ▢ 5 years

D. ▢ 7 years

8. **What is the minimum jail time for a second DUI conviction in Ohio?**

A. ▢ 10 days

B. ▢ 30 days

C. ▢ 60 days

D. ▢ 90 days

9. **Can you refuse a breathalyzer test in Ohio during a DUI investigation?**

A. ▢ Yes

B. ▢ No

C. ▢ Only if you have a valid medical reason

D. ▢ Only if you are under 21 years old

10. What is the legal limit for THC (the active ingredient in marijuana) in a driver's blood in Ohio?

A. ▢ 0.05 ng/mL

B. ▢ 0.08 ng/mL

C. ▢ 0.10 ng/mL

D. ▢ 0.15 ng/mL

11. What is the legal drinking age in Ohio?

A. ▢ 16

B. ▢ 18

C. ▢ 21

D. ▢ 25

12. What is the minimum age to purchase tobacco products in Ohio?

A. ▢ 18

B. ▢ 19

C. ▢ 20

D. ▢ 21

13. What is the penalty for driving under the influence (DUI) of drugs in Ohio

A. ▢ Jail time

B. ▢ Fines

C. ▢ Community service

D. ▢ All of the above

14. What is the penalty for driving under the influence (DUI) of drugs that results in a fatal accident in Ohio?

A. ▢ Imprisonment

B. ▢ Lifetime license suspension

C. ▢ Community service

D. ▢ All of the above

15. What is the legal blood alcohol concentration (BAC) limit for driving in Ohio?

A. ▢ 0.05%

B. ▢ 0.08%

C. ▢ 0.10%

D. ▢ 0.12%

Correct answers for alcohol and drugs exam

1. **B.** 0.08%

2. **B.** $1,000 fine and 1-year license suspension

3. **D.** Increased focus

4. **A.** Yes

5. **D.** $15,000

6. **C.** Increased focus

7. **D.** 7 years

8. **B.** 30 days

9. **B.** No

10. **B.** 0.08 ng/mL

11. **C.** 21

12. **D.** 21

13. **D.** All of the above

14. **D.** All of the above

15. **B.** 0.08%

Alcohol and drugs exam 2

1. **What is the primary ingredient in alcohol that causes its effects on the body and mind?**

    A. ▢ Ethanol

    B. ▢ Methanol

    C. ▢ Isopropanol

    D. ▢ Propanol

2. **What is the legal age to purchase and consume alcohol in Ohio?**

    A. ▢ 18 years old

    B. ▢ 19 years old

    C. ▢ 21 years old

    D. ▢ 25 years old

3. **What is the penalty for providing alcohol to a minor in Ohio?**

    A. ▢ $500 fine

    B. ▢ 6 months in jail

    C. ▢ 1 year in jail

    D. ▢ 2 years in jail

4. **What is the most commonly abused drug in the world?**

    A. ▢ Marijuana

    B. ▢ Cocaine

    C. ▢ Heroin

    D. ▢ Alcohol

5. **Is it illegal to drive under the influence of drugs in Ohio?**

A. ▫ Yes

B. ▫ No

C. ▫ It depends on the prescription

D. ▫ It depends on the circumstances

6. **What is the maximum penalty for drug trafficking in Ohio?**

A. ▫ $1,000 fine

B. ▫ 5 years in jail

C. ▫ 10 years in jail

D. ▫ Life imprisonment

7. **Can you be charged with a DUI for driving under the influence of over-the-counter drugs in Ohio?**

A. ▫ Yes

B. ▫ No

C. ▫ It depends on the prescription

D. ▫ It depends on the circumstances

8. **What is the maximum penalty for possession of drugs in Ohio?**

A. ▫ $1,000 fine

B. ▫ 1 year in jail

C. ▫ 2 years in jail

D. ▫ 5 years in jail

9. **What is the penalty for selling drugs in Ohio?**

A. ▫ $500 fine

B. ▫ 2 years in jail

C. ▫ 5 years in jail

D. □ Life imprisonment

10. What is the maximum penalty for a first-time DUI offense in Ohio?

A. □ 6 months in jail

B. □ 1 year in jail

C. □ 2 years in jail

D. □ 5 years in jail

11. What is the primary ingredient in marijuana that causes its effects on the body and mind?

A. □ THC

B. □ CBD

C. □ CBN

D. □ CBC

12. Is it possible to become addicted to marijuana?

A. □ Yes

B. □ No

C. □ It depends on the person

D. □ It depends on the frequency of use

13. What is the legal age to purchase and consume alcohol in the United States?

A. □ 18 years old

B. □ 19 years old

C. □ 21 years old

D. □ 25 years old

14. What is the penalty for driving under the influence of drugs or alcohol in the United States?

A. ▢ $500 fine

B. ▢ 6 months in jail

C. ▢ 1 year in jail

D. ▢ It varies by state

15. Can you become addicted to prescription drugs?

A. ▢ Yes

B. ▢ No

C. ▢ It depends on the drug

D. ▢ It depends on the person

Correct answers for alcohol and drugs exam 2

1. **A.** Ethanol
2. **C.** 21 years old
3. **D.** 2 years in jail
4. **D.** Alcohol
5. **A.** Yes
6. **D.** Life imprisonment
7. **A.** Yes
8. **D.** 5 years in jail
9. **D.** Life imprisonment
10. **B.** 1 year in jail
11. **A.** THC
12. **A.** Yes
13. **C.** 21 years old
14. **D.** It varies by state
15. **A.** Yes

.

Alcohol and drugs exam 3

1. **Can long-term alcohol abuse lead to brain damage?**

   A. ▢ Yes

   B. ▢ No

   C. ▢ It depends on the person

   D. ▢ It depends on the amount consumed

2. **Can long-term alcohol abuse lead to liver damage?**

   A. ▢ Yes

   B. ▢ No

   C. ▢ It depends on the person

   D. ▢ It depends on the amount consumed

3. **What is the most commonly abused drug in the United States?**

   A. ▢ Marijuana

   B. ▢ Cocaine

   C. ▢ Prescription drugs

   D. ▢ Heroin

4. **What is the process by which the body breaks down alcohol?**

   A. ▢ Hydration

   B. ▢ Digestion

   C. ▢ Metabolism

   D. ▢ Excretion

5. **What is the short-term effect of marijuana use on the brain?**

A. ▢ Increased focus

B. ▢ Decreased appetite

C. ▢ Altered judgment and coordination

D. ▢ Improved memory

6. **What is the medical use of opioid drugs?**

A. ▢ To relieve pain

B. ▢ To treat anxiety

C. ▢ To induce sleep

D. ▢ To cure cancer

7. **What is the most commonly abused prescription drug in the United States?**

A. ▢ Oxycodone

B. ▢ Hydrocodone

C. ▢ Fentanyl

D. ▢ Xanax

8. **What is the most effective way to prevent drunk driving?**

A. ▢ Designating a sober driver

B. ▢ Taking public transportation

C. ▢ Sleeping it off

D. ▢ Drinking coffee

9. **What is the long-term effect of alcohol use on the liver?**

A. ▢ Improved function

B. ▢ Increased production of bile

C. □ Cirrhosis

D. □ Regeneration of damaged tissue

10. What is the short-term effect of cocaine use on the heart?

A. □ Decreased heart rate

B. □ Increased heart rate

C. □ Improved blood flow

D. □ No effect

11. What is the long-term effect of methamphetamine use on the brain?

A. □ Improved cognitive function

B. □ Increased memory

C. □ Decreased dopamine levels

D. □ No effect

12. What is the most commonly abused stimulant drug?

A. □ Methamphetamine

B. □ Cocaine

C. □ Adderall

D. □ Ritalin

13. What is the main ingredient in beer that causes a person to become intoxicated?

A. □ Carbonation

B. □ Sugar

C. □ Alcohol

D. □ Hops

14. What is the short-term effect of opioid use on breathing?

A. ▢ Increased breathing rate

B. ▢ Decreased breathing rate

C. ▢ No effect on breathing rate

D. ▢ Improved breathing quality

15. What is the medical use of benzodiazepines?

A. ▢ To treat depression

B. ▢ To relieve pain

C. ▢ To treat anxiety and insomnia

D. ▢ To cure cancer

Correct answers for alcohol and drugs exam 3

1. **A.** Yes
2. **A.** Yes
3. **C.** Prescription drugs
4. **C.** Metabolism
5. **C.** Altered judgment and coordination
6. **A.** To relieve pain
7. **A.** Oxycodone
8. **A.** Designating a sober driver
9. **C.** Cirrhosis
10. **B.** Increased heart rate
11. **C.** Decreased dopamine levels
12. **C.** Adderall
13. **C.** Alcohol
14. **B.** Decreased breathing rate
15. **C.** To treat anxiety and insomnia

Alcohol and drugs exam 4

1. **What is the legal blood alcohol concentration (BAC) limit in Ohio for drivers under the age of 21?**

   A. ▢ 0.08%

   B. ▢ 0.02%

   C. ▢ 0.05%

   D. ▢ 0.03%

2. **What is the effect of combining alcohol and drugs?**

   A. ▢ It increases the effect of both substances

   B. ▢ It decreases the effect of both substances

   C. ▢ It has no effect on either substance

   D. ▢ It depends on the type of drugs and alcohol involved

3. **What should you do if you see someone who is under the influence of drugs or alcohol attempting to drive?**

   A. ▢ Offer them a ride home

   B. ▢ Ignore them and let them drive

   C. ▢ Call the police

   D. ▢ Confront them and try to stop them from driving

4. **Can you drive under the influence of prescription drugs?**

   A. ▢ Yes, as long as you have a prescription

   B. ▢ No, it's illegal even with a prescription

   C. ▢ Yes, if you feel okay to drive

   D. ▢ No, only if the drugs have warning labels against operating heavy machinery

5. **What is the legal blood alcohol concentration (BAC) limit in Ohio for commercial drivers?**

A. ▢ 0.08%

B. ▢ 0.02%

C. ▢ 0.05%

D. ▢ 0.04%

6. **What are the consequences of driving under the influence of drugs or alcohol in Ohio?**

A. ▢ Fines and jail time

B. ▢ Suspension of driver's license

C. ▢ Community service

D. ▢ All of the above

7. **Can you refuse a chemical test (breathalyzer or blood test) if you are pulled over on suspicion of drunk driving in Ohio?**

A. ▢ Yes, it's your constitutional right

B. ▢ No, it's against the law

C. ▢ Yes, but you will face automatic penalties

D. ▢ No, but you can request a different type of test

8. **What should you do if you are taking prescription drugs that can affect your driving?**

A. ▢ Stop taking the drugs before driving

B. ▢ Drive carefully and avoid roads with heavy traffic

C. ▢ Drink alcohol to counteract the effect of the drugs

D. ▢ Consult a doctor for advice on whether it's safe to drive

9. **What is the legal blood alcohol concentration (BAC) limit in Ohio for drivers over the age of 21 who are operating a boat?**

A. ▢ 0.08%

B. ▢ 0.02%

C. ▢ 0.05%

D. ▢ 0.10%

10. What are the signs of drug impairment while driving?

A. ▢ Slowed reaction time

B. ▢ Poor judgment

C. ▢ Drowsiness

D. ▢ All of the above

11. What is the legal blood alcohol concentration (BAC) limit in Ohio for drivers under the age of 21 who are operating a boat?

A. ▢ 0.08%

B. ▢ 0.02%

C. ▢ 0.05%

D. ▢ 0.10%

12. Can you be arrested for driving under the influence of drugs or alcohol if you are under the legal BAC limit in Ohio?

A. ▢ Yes, if your driving is impaired

B. ▢ No, as long as your BAC is under the limit

C. ▢ Yes, if you are caught with drugs in your system

D. ▢ No, unless you are also breaking another law

13. What are the consequences of refusing a chemical test in Ohio?

A. ▢ Automatic suspension of driver's license

B. ▢ Fines and jail time

C. ▢ Community service

D. ▢ All of the above

14. Can you drive under the influence of over-the-counter medications in Ohio?

A. ▢ Yes, if you follow the recommended dosage

B. ▢ No, it's illegal even if you have a prescription

C. ▢ Yes, if the medication does notimpair your driving

D. ▢ No, if the medication has warning labels against operating heavy machinery

15. What should you do if you are pulled over on suspicion of driving under the influence of drugs or alcohol in Ohio?

A. ▢ Refuse to take a chemical test

B. ▢ Cooperate with the police and answer questions truthfully

C. ▢ Try to talk your way out of the situation

D. ▢ Resist arrest and argue with the police

Correct answers for alcohol and drugs exam 4

1. **B.** 0.02%

2. **A.** It increases the effect of both substances

3. **C.** Call the police

4. **B.** No, it's illegal even with a prescription

5. **D.** 0.04%

6. **D.** All of the above

7. **C.** Yes, but you will face automatic penalties

8. **D.** Consult a doctor for advice on whether it's safe to drive

9. **A.** 0.08%

10. **D.** All of the above

11. **B.** 0.02%

12. **A.** Yes, if your driving is impaired

13. **A.** Automatic suspension of driver's license

14. **C.** Yes, if the medication does not impair your driving

15. **B.** Cooperate with the police and answer questions truthfully

Alcohol and drugs exam 5

1. **What is the legal blood alcohol concentration (BAC) limit in Ohio for drivers over the age of 21 who are operating a motor vehicle?**

    A. ▢ 0.08%

    B. ▢ 0.02%

    C. ▢ 0.05%

    D. ▢ 0.10%

2. **Can you be charged with driving under the influence of drugs if you have a valid prescription for the drug?**

    A. ▢ Yes, if the drug impairs your driving

    B. ▢ No, as long as you have a prescription

    C. ▢ Yes, if the drug is illegal

    D. ▢ No, if the prescription was obtained from a licensed doctor

3. **What is the minimum jail time for a first-time drunk driving conviction in Ohio?**

    A. ▢ 24 hours

    B. ▢ 48 hours

    C. ▢ 72 hours

    D. ▢ None, only fines are imposed

4. **What is the maximum fine for a first-time drunk driving conviction in Ohio?**

    A. ▢ $1000

    B. ▢ $2000

    C. ▢ $3000

    D. ▢ $5000

5. Can a driver in Ohio be charged with drunk driving if they are driving under the influence of drugs other than alcohol?

A. ▢ No, only alcohol-related charges are applied

B. ▢ Yes, if the drug impairs the driver's ability to operate a vehicle safely

C. ▢ No, if the drug is legal

D. ▢ Yes, if the driver tests positive for drugs in a chemical test Answer: B. Yes, if the drug impairs the driver's ability to operate a vehicle safely

6. What is the process by which the liver metabolizes alcohol?

A. ▢ Oxidation

B. ▢ Reduction

C. ▢ Hydrolysis

D. ▢ Deamination

7. What is the active ingredient in marijuana that produces the "high" sensation?

A. ▢ THC

B. ▢ CBD

C. ▢ LSD

D. ▢ PCP

8. What is the term for the combination of alcohol and another drug, such as prescription medication or illicit drugs?

A. ▢ Overdose

B. ▢ Intoxication

C. ▢ Polydrug use

D. ▢ Substance abuse

9. **What is the most severe form of alcohol use disorder, also known as alcoholism?**

A. ▢ Binge drinking

B. ▢ Hazardous drinking

C. ▢ Alcohol dependence

D. ▢ Alcohol abuse

10. **What type of drug is commonly used as a sedative and for the treatment of anxiety and sleep disorders?**

A. ▢ Cocaine

B. ▢ Marijuana

C. ▢ Heroin

D. ▢ Benzodiazepines

11. **What is the name for the symptoms experienced by an individual who has stopped using a substance after using it regularly for a prolonged period of time?**

A. ▢ Overdose

B. ▢ Withdrawal

C. ▢ Intoxication

D. ▢ Substance abuse

12. **What is the term for the practice of consuming large amounts of alcohol in a short period of time?**

A. ▢ Binge drinking

B. ▢ Hazardous drinking

C. ▢ Alcohol dependence

D. ▢ Alcohol abuse

13. **What is the primary active ingredient in hallucinogenic drugs such as LSD and psilocybin (magic mushrooms)?**

A. ▢ THC

B. ▢ CBD

C. ▢ LSD

D. ▢ PCP

14. **What is the term for the repeated use of drugs despite the negative consequences it may have on a person's health, relationships, or daily life?**

A. ▢ Overdose

B. ▢ Intoxication

C. ▢ Substance dependence

D. ▢ Substance abuse

15. **What is the name of the drug commonly referred to as "meth"?**

A. ▢ Methamphetamine

B. ▢ Cocaine

C. ▢ Heroin

D. ▢ Prescription opioids

Correct answers for alcohol and drugs exam 5

1. **A.** 0.08%

2. **A.** Yes, if the drug impairs your driving

3. **B.** 48 hours

4. **D.** $5000

5. **B.** Yes, if the drug impairs the driver's ability to operate a vehicle safely

6. **A.** Oxidation

7. **A.** THC

8. **C.** Polydrug use

9. **C.** Alcohol dependence

10. **D.** Benzodiazepines

11. **B.** Withdrawal

12. **A.** Binge drinking

13. **C.** LSD

14. **D.** Substance abuse

15. **A.** Methamphetamine

Vehicle equipment and maintenance

Vehicle equipment and maintenance are critical aspects of operating a motor vehicle safely and responsibly on the roadways. The Ohio Department of Motor Vehicles (DMV) has established strict standards for vehicle equipment and maintenance, which must be followed by all drivers in the state. The Ohio DMV exam, which is taken by new drivers and those seeking a license renewal, tests the knowledge and understanding of these standards to ensure that all drivers are equipped with the information necessary to maintain their vehicles in a safe and operational condition.

Vehicle equipment refers to the various components that make up a motor vehicle, including the tires, brakes, lights, mirrors, and horns, among others. It is essential to understand the proper functioning and maintenance of each of these components, as they play a crucial role in ensuring the safe operation of a vehicle on the roadways. In Ohio, the DMV has outlined specific equipment standards that must be met by all vehicles, and it is the responsibility of the driver to make sure that their vehicle is in compliance.

Maintenance, on the other hand, refers to the ongoing upkeep of a vehicle to ensure its proper functioning and longevity. This includes regular check-ups and tune-ups, as well as repairs and replacements as needed. Proper vehicle maintenance is critical to maintaining the safety and reliability of a vehicle on the roadways, and it is the responsibility of the driver to keep their vehicle in good working order.

The Ohio DMV exam covers a variety of topics related to vehicle equipment and maintenance, including proper tire inflation, brake maintenance, and the functioning of lights and signals. The exam also includes questions about the role of the driver in maintaining their vehicle, including the importance of regularly checking fluid levels and conducting regular maintenance check-ups.

In addition to the knowledge required to pass the Ohio DMV exam, it is important for all drivers to understand the legal and practical implications of maintaining their vehicles. This includes staying current with state and federal regulations, as well as adhering to best practices for safe and responsible driving. For example, it is against the law in Ohio to operate a vehicle with defective equipment, and drivers can be fined or face legal consequences if they are found to be in violation of the equipment standards outlined by the DMV.

Furthermore, proper vehicle maintenance is essential not only for the safety of the driver and passengers, but also for other drivers on the roadways. A well-maintained vehicle is less likely to experience mechanical failures or other problems that could cause an accident or put other drivers at risk. In addition, properly maintained vehicles tend to be more fuel efficient and have a longer lifespan, which can save drivers time, money, and resources in the long run.

In this chapter, we will explore the key components of vehicle equipment and maintenance, including the standards outlined by the Ohio DMV, the role of the driver in maintaining their vehicle, and the importance of proper vehicle maintenance in ensuring the safety of all drivers on the roadways. We will delve into the different components of a vehicle, including the tires, brakes, lights, and mirrors, and discuss the proper maintenance and upkeep required to keep these components functioning properly. We will also review some of the common questions that appear on the Ohio DMV exam, providing a comprehensive overview of the knowledge and understanding required to pass the exam and become a safe and responsible driver. Additionally, we will explore the legal and practical implications of vehicle maintenance, including the consequences of operating a vehicle with defective equipment and the benefits of maintaining a vehicle in good working order.

For training purposes, you can mark the ▢ symbol next to what you think is the correct answer: Once you have chosen the correct answer, use a pencil or pen to mark the ▢ symbol next to that answer.

Vehicle equipment and maintenance exam

1. **What is the minimum tread depth required for tires in Ohio?**

    A. ▢ 4/32 of an inch

    B. ▢ 2/32 of an inch

    C. ▢ 6/32 of an inch

    D. ▢ 8/32 of an inch

2. **What type of lighting is required on the front of a vehicle in Ohio during the day?**

    A. ▢ Yellow

    B. ▢ White

    C. ▢ Red

    D. ▢ Blue

3. **How often should a driver check their tire pressure?**

    A. ▢ Every month

    B. ▢ Every 3 months

    C. ▢ Every 6 months

    D. ▢ Every year

4. **What is the minimum stopping distance for a vehicle traveling at 60 mph in dry conditions?**

    A. ▢ 120 feet

    B. ▢ 150 feet

    C. ▢ 175 feet

    D. ▢ 200 feet

5. **How often should a driver have their brakes inspected?**

A. ☐ Every year

B. ☐ Every 2 years

C. ☐ Every 3 years

D. ☐ Every 4 years

6. **What is the purpose of a horn in a vehicle?**

A. ☐ To signal to other drivers

B. ☐ To scare animals off the road

C. ☐ To play music

D. ☐ To create a noise

7. **What type of lighting is required on the rear of a vehicle in Ohio during the day?**

A. ☐ Yellow

B. ☐ White

C. ☐ Red

D. ☐ Blue

8. **What is the minimum number of mirrors required on a vehicle in Ohio?**

A. ☐ 1

B. ☐ 2

C. ☐ 3

D. ☐ 4

9. **How often should a driver check their fluid levels?**

A. ☐ Every month

B. ▢ Every 3 months

C. ▢ Every 6 months

D. ▢ Every year

10. What is the purpose of conducting regular maintenance check-ups on a vehicle?

A. ▢ To maintain the safety and reliability of the vehicle

B. ▢ To improve fuel efficiency

C. ▢ To increase the lifespan of the vehicle

D. ▢ All of the above

11. What is the purpose of a vehicle's air filter?

A. ▢ To improve engine performance

B. ▢ To reduce fuel consumption

C. ▢ To protect the engine from dirt and dust

D. ▢ To improve the vehicle's sound system

12. What should you check before a long road trip to ensure your vehicle is in good condition?

A. ▢ Engine oil level

B. ▢ Brake fluid level

C. ▢ Tire pressure

D. ▢ All of the above

13. What is the recommended tire pressure for a vehicle?

A. ▢ The pressure listed on the tire

B. ▢ The pressure listed in the vehicle owner's manual

C. ▢ The maximum pressure listed on the tire

D. ▢ The minimum pressure listed on the tire

14. What is the purpose of a vehicle's power steering system?

A. ▢ To provide additional horsepower to the engine

B. ▢ To make steering easier at low speeds

C. ▢ To reduce road noise

D. ▢ To improve the vehicle's fuel efficiency

15. What should you do if the check engine light comes on while you are driving?

A. ▢ Ignore it

B. ▢ Continue driving normally

C. ▢ Have the vehicle inspected as soon as possible

D. ▢ Turn off the engine and coast to a stop

Correct answers for vehicle equipment and maintenance exam

1. **C.** 6/32 of an inch
2. **B.** White
3. **A.** Every month
4. **B.** 150 feet
5. **A.** Every year
6. **A.** To signal to other drivers
7. **C.** Red
8. **B.** 2
9. **A.** Every month
10. **D.** All of the above
11. **C.** To protect the engine from dirt and dust
12. **D.** All of the above
13. **B.** The pressure listed in the vehicle owner's manual
14. **B.** To make steering easier at low speeds
15. **C.** Have the vehicle inspected as soon as possible

Vehicle equipment and maintenance exam 2

1. What is the recommended interval for changing the engine oil in a vehicle?

A. ▢ Every 6 months

B. ▢ Every 12 months

C. ▢ Every 3,000 miles

D. ▢ It varies, consult the vehicle owner's manual

2. What is the function of a catalytic converter in a vehicle?

A. ▢ Increases fuel efficiency

B. ▢ Reduces emissions

C. ▢ Improves suspension

D. ▢ Enhances engine performance

3. What should you check before a long road trip to ensure your vehicle is in good working condition?

A. ▢ Engine oil level

B. ▢ Battery charge

C. ▢ Brake fluid level

D. ▢ All of the above

4. What type of battery is commonly used in most vehicles?

A. ▢ Lead-acid battery

B. ▢ Lithium-ion battery

C. ▢ Nickel-cadmium battery

D. ▢ Alkaline battery

5. What is the recommended tire pressure for a vehicle?

    A. ▢ The pressure indicated on the tire sidewall

    B. ▢ The pressure indicated in the owner's manual

    C. ▢ The pressure indicated on the gas pump dispenser

    D. ▢ The maximum pressure indicated on the tire sidewal

6. How often should you change the oil in your vehicle?

    A. ▢ Every 3,000 miles

    B. ▢ Every 5,000 miles

    C. ▢ Every 7,500 miles

    D. ▢ The frequency of oil changes depends on various factors such as driving conditions, type of oil used, and vehicle manufacturer recommendations.

7. What is the purpose of a cabin air filter in a vehicle?

    A. ▢ To regulate engine temperature

    B. ▢ To filter and clean the air entering the cabin

    C. ▢ To improve soundproofing

    D. ▢ To enhance engine performance

8. What is the function of a power steering pump in a vehicle?

    A. ▢ Increases engine power

    B. ▢ Regulates air conditioning

    C. ▢ Helps to steer the vehicle more easily

    D. ▢ Maintains battery charge

9. What is the recommended service interval for brake pads in a vehicle?

    A. ▢ Every 6 months

    B. ▢ Every 12 months

    C. ▢ Every 24 months

    D. ▢ The service interval depends on various factors such as driving conditions, brake usage, and vehicle manufacturer recommendations

10. What type of oil should you use in your vehicle's engine?

    A. ▢ Synthetic oil

    B. ▢ Mineral oil

    C. ▢ The type of oil depends on various factors such as driving conditions, climate, and vehicle manufacturer recommendations.

    D. ▢ Any type of oil

11. What is the purpose of a drive belt in a vehicle?

    A. ▢ Transmits power from the engine to the alternator

    B. ▢ Regulates engine temperature

    C. ▢ Improves suspension

    D. ▢ Enhances engine performance

12. What is the function of the spark plugs in a vehicle?

    A. ▢ Ignites fuel to power the engine

    B. ▢ Regulates engine temperature

    C. ▢ Improves suspension

    D. ▢ Increases engine performance

13. What is the function of a transmission in a vehicle?

A. ▢ Generates power for the engin

B. ▢ Transmits power from the engine to the wheels

C. ▢ Regulates air conditioning

D. ▢ Maintains battery charge

14. What is the recommended tire pressure for a vehicle?

A. ▢ The pressure indicated on the tire sidewall

B. ▢ The pressure indicated in the owner's manual

C. ▢ The pressure indicated on the gas pump dispenser

D. ▢ The maximum pressure indicated on the tire sidewall

15. What is the purpose of a muffler in a vehicle?

A. ▢ Reduces engine noise

B. ▢ Increases engine performance

C. ▢ Regulates engine temperature

D. ▢ Improves suspension

Correct answers for Vehicle equipment and maintenance exam 2

1. **D.** It varies, consult the vehicle owner's manual

2. **B.** Reduces emissions

3. **D.** All of the above

4. **A.** Lead-acid battery

5. **B.** The pressure indicated in the owner's manual

6. **D.** The frequency of oil changes depends on various factors such as driving conditions, type of oil used, and vehicle manufacturer recommendations.

7. **B.** To filter and clean the air entering the cabin

8. **C.** Helps to steer the vehicle more easily

9. **D.** The service interval depends on various factors such as driving conditions, brake usage, and vehicle manufacturer recommendations.

10. **C.** The type of oil depends on various factors such as driving conditions, climate, and vehicle manufacturer recommendations.

11. **A.** Transmits power from the engine to the alternator

12. **A.** Ignites fuel to power the engine

13. **B.** Transmits power from the engine to the wheels

14. **B.** The pressure indicated in the owner's manual

15. **A.** Reduces engine noise

Vehicle equipment and maintenance exam 3

1. What is the purpose of a radiator in a vehicle?

    A. ▢ Increases fuel efficiency

    B. ▢ Reduces emissions

    C. ▢ Regulates engine temperature

    D. ▢ Enhances engine performance

2. What type of brake system is commonly used in most vehicles?

    A. ▢ Disc brakes

    B. ▢ Drum brakes

    C. ▢ Both disc and drum brakes

    D. ▢ Neither disc nor drum brakes

3. What is the recommended service interval for a vehicle's air filter?

    A. ▢ Every 6 months

    B. ▢ Every 12 months

    C. ▢ Every 24 months

    D. ▢ The service interval depends on various factors such as driving conditions, climate, and vehicle manufacturer recommendations.

4. What is the function of a fuel pump in a vehicle?

    A. ▢ Regulates engine temperature

    B. ▢ Delivers fuel to the engine

    C. ▢ Improves suspension

    D. ▢ Increases engine performance

5. What is the purpose of a catalytic converter in a vehicle?

    A. ▢ Reduces emissions

    B. ▢ Improves fuel efficiency

    C. ▢ Regulates engine temperature

    D. ▢ Increases engine performance

6. What type of oil filter is commonly used in most vehicles?

    A. ▢ Cartridge oil filter

    B. ▢ Spin-on oil filter

    C. ▢ Both cartridge and spin-on oil filters

    D. ▢ Neither cartridge nor spin-on oil filters

7. What is the recommended service interval for a vehicle's transmission fluid?

    A. ▢ Every 6 months

    B. ▢ Every 12 months

    C. ▢ Every 24 months

    D. ▢ The service interval depends on various factors such as driving conditions, transmission usage, and vehicle manufacturer recommendations.

8. What is the purpose of a shock absorber in a vehicle?

    A. ▢ Enhances suspension

    B. ▢ Regulates engine temperature

    C. ▢ Increases engine performance

    D. ▢ Reduces emissions

9. What type of engine oil is recommended for high-performance vehicles?

A. ▫ Synthetic oil

B. ▫ Mineral oil

C. ▫ The type of oil depends on various factors such as driving conditions, climate, and vehicle manufacturer recommendations.

D. ▫ Synthetic oil

10. What is the function of a starter motor in a vehicle?

A. ▫ Powers the vehicle's electrical system

B. ▫ Starts the engine

C. ▫ Regulates engine temperature

D. ▫ Increases engine performance

11. What is the recommended service interval for a vehicle's battery?

A. ▫ Every 6 months

B. ▫ Every 12 months

C. ▫ Every 24 months

D. ▫ The service interval depends on various factors such as driving conditions, battery usage, and vehicle manufacturer recommendations.

12. What is the purpose of a muffler in a vehicle?

A. ▫ Reduces emissions

B. ▫ Reduces engine noise

C. ▫ Regulates engine temperature

D. ▫ Enhances engine performance

13. What type of tire is best suited for snowy and icy road conditions?

A. ▢ All-season tires

B. ▢ Summer tires

C. ▢ Winter tires

D. ▢ Performance tires

14. What is the recommended service interval for a vehicle's brake pads?

A. ▢ Every 6 months

B. ▢ Every 12 months

C. ▢ Every 24 months

D. ▢ The service interval depends on various factors such as driving conditions, brake usage, and vehicle manufacturer recommendations.

15. What is the function of a transmission in a vehicle?

A. ▢ Regulates engine temperature

B. ▢ Powers the wheels

C. ▢ Enhances engine performance

D. ▢ Reduces emissions

Correct answers for vehicle equipment and maintenance exam 3

1. **C.** Regulates engine temperature
2. **C.** Both disc and drum brake
3. **D.** The service interval depends on various factors such as driving conditions, climate, and vehicle manufacturer recommendations.
4. **B.** Delivers fuel to the engine
5. **A.** Reduces emissions
6. **B.** Spin-on oil filter
7. **D.** The service interval depends on various factors such as driving conditions, transmission usage, and vehicle manufacturer recommendations.
8. **A.** Enhances suspension
9. **A.** Synthetic oil
10. **B.** Starts the engine
11. **D.** The service interval depends on various factors such as driving conditions, battery usage, and vehicle manufacturer recommendations.
12. **B.** Reduces engine noise
13. **C.** Winter tires
14. **D.** The service interval depends on various factors such as driving conditions, brake usage, and vehicle manufacturer recommendations.
15. **B.** Powers the wheels

Vehicle equipment and maintenance exam 4

1. **What is the function of a car's air filter?**

   A. ▢ Increases engine performance

   B. ▢ Prevents engine overheating

   C. ▢ Cleans engine air intake

   D. ▢ Reduces fuel consumptio

2. **What type of engine oil is recommended for most vehicles?**

   A. ▢ Synthetic

   B. ▢ Mineral

   C. ▢ Semi-synthetic

   D. ▢ High mileage

3. **What is the purpose of a timing belt in a vehicle's engine?**

   A. ▢ Transfers power to the wheels

   B. ▢ Maintains engine timing

   C. ▢ Cools the engine

   D. ▢ Lubricates the engine

4. **How often should you check the tire pressure in your vehicle?**

   A. ▢ Monthly

   B. ▢ Weekly

   C. ▢ Daily

   D. ▢ Every time you drive

5. **What does a vehicle's ABS (Anti-Lock Braking System) do?**

A. ▢ Improves fuel efficiency

B. ▢ Enhances driving comfort

C. ▢ Prevents wheel lockup during hard braking

D. ▢ Increases horsepower

6. **What is the recommended frequency for a vehicle's oil change?**

A. ▢ Every 3 months

B. ▢ Every 5,000 miles

C. ▢ Every 10,000 miles

D. ▢ Whenever the oil level decreases

7. **What is the function of a vehicle's transmission?**

A. ▢ Provides power to the wheels

B. ▢ Maintains engine timing

C. ▢ Controls the transfer of power from the engine to the wheels

D. ▢ Enhances driving comfort

8. **What type of battery is commonly used in most vehicles?**

A. ▢ Lithium-ion

B. ▢ Nickel-cadmium

C. ▢ Lead-acid

D. ▢ Alkaline

9. **What is the purpose of a catalytic converter in a vehicle's exhaust system?**

A. ▢ Increases engine power

B. ▢ Reduces exhaust emissions

C. ▢ Improves fuel efficiency

D. ▢ Enhances driving comfort

10. What is the function of a vehicle's power steering system?

A. ▢ Helps turn the wheels with less effort

B. ▢ Increases horsepower

C. ▢ Improves fuel efficiency

D. ▢ Enhances driving comfort

11. What is the recommended frequency for checking the coolant level in a vehicle?

A. ▢ Every 3 months

B. ▢ Every 5,000 miles

C. ▢ Every 10,000 miles

D. ▢ Monthly

12. What is the function of a vehicle's alternator?

A. ▢ Stores energy for later use

B. ▢ Provides power to the electrical system while the engine is running

C. ▢ Increases engine power

D. ▢ Enhances driving comfort

13. What is the purpose of a vehicle's suspension system?

A. ▢ Improves fuel efficiency

B. ▢ Enhances driving comfort and stability

C. ▢ Increases horsepower

D. ▢ Controls engine speed

14. What is the recommended frequency for rotating tires on a vehicle?

A. ▢ Every 5,000 miles

B. ▢ Every 10,000 miles

C. ▢ Every 6 months

D. ▢ Every time you check the tire pressure

15. What is the function of a vehicle's oil pump?

A. ▢ Controls the transfer of power from the engine to the wheels

B. ▢ Lubricates the engine

C. ▢ Provides power to the electrical system while the engine is running

D. ▢ Enhances driving comfort

Correct answers for vehicle equipment and maintenance exam 4

1. **C.** Cleans engine air intake

2. **C.** Semi-synthetic

3. **B.** Maintains engine timing

4. **A.** Monthly

5. **C.** Prevents wheel lockup during hard braking

6. **B.** Every 5,000 miles

7. **C.** Controls the transfer of power from the engine to the wheels

8. **C.** Lead-acid

9. **B.** Reduces exhaust emissions

10. **A.** Helps turn the wheels with less effort

11. **D.** Monthly

12. **B.** Provides power to the electrical system while the engine is running

13. **B.** Enhances driving comfort and stability

14. **A.** Every 5,000 miles

15. **B.** Lubricates the engine

Vehicle equipment and maintenance exam 5

1. **What is the purpose of a vehicle's battery?**

A. ▢ Provides power to the engine

B. ▢ Stores energy for later use

C. ▢ Increases engine power

D. ▢ Enhances driving comfort

2. **What is the recommended frequency for checking the brake pads on a vehicle?**

A. ▢ Every 6 months

B. ▢ Every 5,000 miles

C. ▢ Every 10,000 miles

D. ▢ Monthly

3. **What is the function of a vehicle's exhaust manifold?**

A. ▢ Increases engine power

B. ▢ Collects exhaust gases from the cylinders and routes them to the exhaust system

C. ▢ Improves fuel efficiency

D. ▢ Enhances driving comfort

4. **What is the recommended frequency for checking the air conditioning system in a vehicle?**

A. ▢ Every 6 months

B. ▢ Every 5,000 miles

C. ▢ Every 10,000 miles

D. ▢ Annually

5. **What is the purpose of a vehicle's fuel pump?**

A. ▢ Increases engine power

B. ▢ Delivers fuel from the gas tank to the engine

C. ▢ Improves fuel efficiency

D. ▢ Enhances driving comfort

6. **What is the function of a vehicle's throttle body?**

A. ▢ Controls the amount of air entering the engine

B. ▢ Increases engine power

C. ▢ Improves fuel efficiency

D. ▢ Enhances driving comfort

7. **What is the recommended frequency for checking the wiper blades on a vehicle?**

A. ▢ Every 6 months

B. ▢ Every 5,000 miles

C. ▢ Every 10,000 miles

D. ▢ Annually

8. **What is the main function of a vehicle's muffler?**

A. ▢ To reduce engine noise

B. ▢ To increase engine power

C. ▢ To improve fuel efficiency

D. ▢ To cool the engine

9. **What is the recommended tire pressure for a vehicle with a tire size of 205/55 R16?**

A. ▢ 28 psi

B. ❑ 35 psi

C. ❑ 32 psi

D. ❑ 30 psi

10. What type of oil should be used in a diesel engine?

A. ❑ Synthetic oil

B. ❑ High mileage oil

C. ❑ Conventional oil

D. ❑ Diesel oil

11. How often should you check the brakes on your vehicle?

A. ❑ Every 10,000 miles

B. ❑ Every 5,000 miles

C. ❑ Every 7,500 miles

D. ❑ Every 6 months

12. What type of battery is commonly used in most vehicles?

A. ❑ Nickel-Metal Hydride

B. ❑ Lithium Ion

C. ❑ Lead- Acid

D. ❑ Nickel- Cadmium

13. What is the purpose of a transmission filter in a vehicle?

A. ❑ To prevent contaminants from entering the transmission system

B. ❑ To increase the efficiency of the engine

C. ❑ To reduce the weight of the vehicle

D. ▫ To improve fuel economy

14. When should you perform a wheel alignment on your vehicle?

A. ▫ Every year

B. ▫ Every 10,000 miles

C. ▫ When you notice a problem with the vehicle's handling

D. ▫ When you rotate your tires

15. What type of fuel is recommended for use in a vehicle equipped with a catalytic converter?

A. ▫ Unleaded gasoline

B. ▫ Diesel

C. ▫ Lead-based gasoline

D. ▫ Ethanol-blended gasoline

Correct answers for vehicle equipment and maintenance exam 5

1. **B.** Stores energy for later use

2. **B.** Every 5,000 miles

3. **B.** Collects exhaust gases from the cylinders and routes them to the exhaust system

4. **D.** Annually

5. **B.** Delivers fuel from the gas tank to the engine

6. **A.** Controls the amount of air entering the engine

7. **A.** Every 6 months

8. **A.** To reduce engine noise

9. **C.** 32 psi

10. **D.** Diesel oil

11. **D.** Every 6 months

12. **C.** Lead- Acid

13. **A.** To prevent contaminants from entering the transmission system

14. **C.** When you notice a problem with the vehicle's handling

15. **A.** Unleaded gasoline

Sharing the road

As a driver on Ohio's roads, it is important to understand the concept of sharing the road. This refers to the idea that all road users - including drivers, pedestrians, cyclists, and motorcyclists - must work together to ensure the safety of everyone on the road. To help you become a safe and responsible road user, the Ohio Department of Motor Vehicles (DMV) has included a section on sharing the road on its driver's license examination.

The sharing the road section of the Ohio DMV exam will test your knowledge of the rules and regulations that govern the interactions between different road users. This includes knowledge of traffic signs and signals, as well as a general understanding of the responsibilities of each road user. You will also be tested on your ability to recognize and respond to various road hazards, such as pedestrians, other vehicles, and adverse weather conditions.

In addition to the theoretical knowledge that you will be tested on, the Ohio DMV exam will also assess your practical skills and habits when it comes to sharing the road. This includes your ability to communicate effectively with other road users through signals, gestures, and eye contact, as well as your ability to adjust your speed and position on the road based on the actions of other road users.

It is important to remember that sharing the road is not just about following the rules and regulations - it is also about being aware of the needs and actions of other road users, and working together to create a safe and efficient road environment for everyone. Whether you are a seasoned driver or a new learner, understanding the concepts of sharing the road is essential for becoming a safe and responsible road user in Ohio.

For training purposes, you can mark the ▢ symbol next to what you think is the correct answer: Once you have chosen the correct answer, use a pencil or pen to mark the ▢ symbol next to that answer.

Sharing the road exam

1. **What is the proper speed limit for a residential area in Ohio?**

    A. ▢ 25 mph

    B. ▢ 35 mph

    C. ▢ 45 mph

    D. ▢ 55 mph

2. **What should you do when approaching a pedestrian who is crossing the street?**

    A. ▢ Ignore them and continue driving

    B. ▢ Honk your horn to scare them off the road

    C. ▢ Slow down and allow them to cross safely

    D. ▢ Speed up to get past them quickly

3. **What is the proper action to take when encountering a bicycle on the road?**

    A. ▢ Drive as close as possible to the bicycle

    B. ▢ Pass the bicycle quickly

    C. ▢ Allow the bicycle at least 3 feet of space when passing

    D. ▢ Honk your horn to let the cyclist know you are there

4. **What is the proper action to take when approaching a stopped school bus with its red lights flashing?**

    A. ▢ Pass the bus quickly

    B. ▢ Slow down and prepare to stop

    C. ▢ Honk your horn to let the bus know you are there

    D. ▢ Drive around the bus

5. **What is the proper speed limit for a highway in Ohio?**

A. ▢ 55 mph

B. ▢ 65 mph

C. ▢ 75 mph

D. ▢ 85 mph

6. **What should you do when approaching an intersection with a yield sign?**

A. ▢ Stop and wait for all other vehicles to go first

B. ▢ Slow down and be prepared to stop if necessary

C. ▢ Speed up to beat other vehicles through the intersection

D. ▢ Ignore the yield sign and continue driving

7. **What should you do when approaching a roundabout?**

A. ▢ Drive as fast as possible through the roundabout

B. ▢ Slow down and yield to any vehicles already in the roundabout

C. ▢ Drive on the left side of the roundabout

D. ▢ Ignore other vehicles and continue driving

8. **What is the proper action to take when encountering a stopped emergency vehicle with its lights flashing?**

A. ▢ Drive around the emergency vehicle

B. ▢ Slow down and move over to the next lane if possible

C. ▢ Speed up to get past the emergency vehicle quickly

D. ▢ Ignore the emergency vehicle and continue driving

9. **What should you do when encountering a funeral procession on the road?**

A. ☐ Drive as fast as possible to get past the procession

B. ☐ Ignore the procession and continue driving

C. ☐ Slow down and allow the procession to proceed through the intersection first

D. ☐ Speed up to get ahead of the procession

10. What is the proper action to take when encountering a cyclist riding in the same direction as your vehicle?

A. ☐ Drive as close as possible to the cyclist

B. ☐ Pass the cyclist quickly

C. ☐ Allow the cyclist at least 3 feet of space when passing

D. ☐ Honk your horn to let the cyclist know you are there

11. What should you do when you approach a school bus with its stop sign arm extended?

A. ☐ Pass the school bus on the right side

B. ☐ Slow down and prepare to stop

C. ☐ Drive around the school bus as quickly as possible

D. ☐ Honk your horn to let the school bus driver know you are there

12. What is the proper action to take when encountering a funeral procession?

A. ☐ Drive as quickly as possible through the procession

B. ☐ Slow down and be respectful of the procession

C. ☐ Drive around the procession using the shoulder

D. ☐ Honk your horn to let the procession know you are ther

13. What should you do when approaching a road with a flashing yellow light?

A. ☐ Stop and wait for the light to turn green

B. ☐ Slow down and proceed with caution

C. ▢ Drive through the intersection as quickly as possible

D. ▢ Honk your horn to let other drivers know you are there

14. What is the proper speed limit for a highway in Ohio?

A. ▢ 25 mph

B. ▢ 35 mph

C. ▢ 55 mph

D. ▢ 65 mph

15. What should you do when approaching a stopped emergency vehicle with its lights flashing?

A. ▢ Drive around the emergency vehicle

B. ▢ Slow down and move over to the next lane if possible

C. ▢ Speed up to get past the emergency vehicle quickly

D. ▢ Ignore the emergency vehicle and continue driving

Correct answers for sharing the road exam

1. **A.** 25 mph

2. **C.** Slow down and allow them to cross safely

3. **C.** Allow the bicycle at least 3 feet of space when passing

4. **B.** Slow down and prepare to stop

5. **B.** 65 mph

6. **B.** Slow down and be prepared to stop if necessary

7. **B.** Slow down and yield to any vehicles already in the roundabout

8. **B.** Slow down and move over to the next lane if possible

9. **C.** Slow down and allow the procession to proceed through the intersection first

10. **C.** Allow the cyclist at least 3 feet of space when passing

11. **B.** Slow down and prepare to stop

12. **B.** Slow down and be respectful of the procession

13. **B.** Slow down and proceed with caution

14. **D.** 65 mph

15. **B.** Slow down and move over to the next lane if possible

Sharing the road exam 2

1. **When a pedestrian is crossing the road, what should a driver do?**

    A. ▢ Speed up to pass quickly

    B. ▢ Stop and yield the right of way

    C. ▢ Honk loudly to get their attention

    D. ▢ Drive around them

2. **If you are driving on a road with two or more lanes in the same direction, which lane should you use for passing other vehicles?**

    A. ▢ The right lane

    B. ▢ The left lane

    C. ▢ Any lane that is open

    D. ▢ The center lane

3. **When driving on a road with a speed limit of 55 mph, what is the minimum speed you should drive?**

    A. ▢ 55 mph

    B. ▢ 50 mph

    C. ▢ 60 mph

    D. ▢ There is no minimum speed

4. **At a four-way stop, which vehicle should go first?**

    A. ▢ The vehicle on the right

    B. ▢ The vehicle that arrived first

    C. ▢ The vehicle turning left

D. ▫ The vehicle on the left

5. **When merging onto a highway, you should:**

A. ▫ Drive as fast as possible to get in front of other vehicles

B. ▫ Slow down and wait for an opening in traffic

C. ▫ Change lanes frequently to get ahead of other vehicles

D. ▫ Stop and wait for all traffic to clear

6. **When driving in heavy rain, you should:**

A. ▫ Drive faster than usual to get to your destination quickly

B. ▫ Maintain the same speed as other vehicles

C. ▫ Reduce your speed and increase following distance

D. ▫ Use high beams to see better

7. **If you approach a roundabout, you should:**

A. ▫ Slow down and stop before entering

B. ▫ Yield to vehicles already in the roundabout

C. ▫ Honk your horn loudly to make other drivers aware of your presence

D. ▫ Drive as quickly as possible through the roundabout

8. **When approaching a crosswalk, what should a driver do?**

A. ▫ Increase speed to get across quickly

B. ▫ Stop and yield to pedestrians

C. ▫ Honk loudly to warn pedestrians

D. ▫ Drive around pedestrians

9. **If a driver is tailgating, what should you do?**

A. ▢ Speed up to get away

B. ▢ Brake suddenly to teach them a lesson

C. ▢ Move to another lane if possible

D. ▢ Ignore them

10. When driving in fog, you should:

A. ▢ Use high beams to see better

B. ▢ Drive as fast as possible to get to your destination quickly

C. ▢ Reduce speed and increase following distance

D. ▢ Stop and wait for the fog to clear

11. At an intersection with a flashing yellow light, what should a driver do?

A. ▢ Stop and wait for the light to turn green

B. ▢ Proceed with caution

C. ▢ Yield to pedestrians

D. ▢ Increase speed to get through quickly

12. If a car is flashing its high beams at you, what should you do?

A. ▢ Flash your high beams back

B. ▢ Slow down and pull over

C. ▢ Increase speed to get away

D. ▢ Proceed with caution

13. When passing a cyclist, you should:

A. ▢ Honk loudly to warn them

B. ▫ Pass quickly and closely

C. ▫ Wait for the cyclist to move off the road

D. ▫ Leave a safe distance of at least 3 feet

14. What should you do when approaching a pedestrian crossing the road?

A. ▫ Stop and wait for the pedestrian to cross

B. ▫ Slow down and proceed with caution

C. ▫ Honk the horn to warn the pedestrian

D. ▫ Speed up to pass the pedestrian quickly

15. If a pedestrian is crossing the road outside of a crosswalk, what should a driver do?

A. ▫ Stop and yield the right of way

B. ▫ Drive around them

C. ▫ Honk loudly to get their attention

D. ▫ Increase speed to get past quickly

Correct answers for sharing the road exam 2

1. **B.** Stop and yield the right of way
2. **B.** The left lane
3. **D.** There is no minimum speed
4. **B.** The vehicle that arrived first
5. **B.** Slow down and wait for an opening in traffic
6. **C.** Reduce your speed and increase following distance
7. **B.** Yield to vehicles already in the roundabout
8. **B.** Stop and yield to pedestrians
9. **C.** Move to another lane if possible
10. **C.** Reduce speed and increase following distance
11. **B.** Proceed with caution
12. **D.** Proceed with caution
13. **D.** Leave a safe distance of at least 3 feet
14. **B.** Vehicles already in the roundabout
15. **A.** Stop and yield the right of way

Sharing the road exam 3

1. **When approaching a junction with a roundabout, a driver must give priority to:**

   A. ▢ Pedestrians crossing the road

   B. ▢ Vehicles already in the roundabout

   C. ▢ Vehicles entering the roundabout from the left

   D. ▢ None of the above

2. **When passing a bicycle on the road, what is the minimum safe passing distance?**

   A. ▢ 3 feet

   B. ▢ 5 feet

   C. ▢ 7 feet

   D. ▢ 10 feet

3. **When driving behind a slow-moving vehicle, it is best to:**

   A. ▢ Tailgate to make the vehicle move faster

   B. ▢ Flash your lights to signal the vehicle to pull over

   C. ▢ Pass the vehicle as soon as possible

   D. ▢ Stay a safe distance behind the vehicle

4. **What should you do if you approach a roundabout?**

   A. ▢ Stop and wait for other vehicles to clear

   B. ▢ Yield to any vehicles already in the roundabout

   C. ▢ Use your horn to signal your presence

   D. ▢ Drive as fast as possible through the roundabout

5. If a school bus is stopped ahead of you with its red lights flashing, what should you do?

A. ▢ Slow down and proceed with cautio

B. ▢ Pass the stopped school bus on the right

C. ▢ Stop until the red lights are turned off

D. ▢ Stop only if you're driving in the same direction as the bus

6. When driving in heavy rain, you should:

A. ▢ Drive slower than usual

B. ▢ Turn on your hazard lights

C. ▢ Use high beams to see better

D. ▢ Increase your speed to reach your destination faster

7. When following a truck, you should:

A. ▢ Stay close to the truck to draft behind it

B. ▢ Keep a safe following distance

C. ▢ Pass the truck as soon as possible

D. ▢ Flash your lights to signal the truck to move over

8. If a car ahead of you is signaling to turn left, you should:

A. ▢ Speed up to pass the car before it turns

B. ▢ Stay close to the car to prevent it from turning

C. ▢ Slow down and be prepared to stop

D. ▢ Honk the horn to signal the car to turn

9. When approaching an intersection controlled by a stop sign, you should:

A. ▢ Slow down and proceed with caution

B. □ Stop, then proceed when safe

C. □ Honk your horn to warn other drivers

D. □ Keep driving without stopping

10. When driving on a two-lane road, what should you do when a vehicle is trying to pass you?

A. □ Speed up to prevent the vehicle from passing

B. □ Slow down and move to the right to allow the vehicle to pass

C. □ Flash your lights to signal the passing vehicle

D. □ Move to the left to block the passing vehicle

11. If you are in an accident and are able to move your vehicle, you should:

A. □ Drive away from the scene to avoid the police

B. □ Move your vehicle to the side of the road and turn on your hazard lights

C. □ Leave your vehicle in the middle of the road

D. □ Try to hide your vehicle from view

12. When approaching a pedestrian crossing, a driver must slow down and be prepared to stop if necessary. When may a driver legally proceed without stopping?

A. □ When there is a red light signal

B. □ When the pedestrian has started to cross the road

C. □ When the pedestrian has crossed more than half the road

D. □ When there is no pedestrian present or crossing

13. When a driver approaches a roundabout, they must give way to:

A. □ Pedestrians crossing the road

B. □ Vehicles already in the roundabout

C. □ Vehicles entering the roundabout from the left

D. ▢ None of the above

14. A driver is approaching a stationary emergency vehicle with flashing lights on the side of the road. What should the driver do?

A. ▢ Drive as close as possible to the emergency vehicle

B. ▢ Increase speed and pass the emergency vehicle as quickly as possible

C. ▢ Move over to the left lane, if possible, or slow down

D. ▢ None of the above

15. When approaching a give way sign, a driver must:

A. ▢ Increase speed to beat other traffic

B. ▢ Stop and wait for a gap in the traffic

C. ▢ Drive through the sign without slowing down

D. ▢ None of the above

Correct answers for sharing the road exam 3

1. **A.** Stop and wait for the pedestrian to cross

2. **B.** 5 feet

3. **D.** Stay a safe distance behind the vehicle

4. **B.** Yield to any vehicles already in the roundabout

5. **C.** Stop until the red lights are turned off

6. **A.** Drive slower than usual

7. **B.** Keep a safe following distance

8. **C.** Slow down and be prepared to stop

9. **B.** Stop, then proceed when safe

10. **B.** Slow down and move to the right to allow the vehicle to pass

11. **B.** Move your vehicle to the side of the road and turn on your hazard lights

12. **D.** When there is no pedestrian present or crossing

13. **B.** Vehicles already in the roundabout

14. **C.** Move over to the left lane, if possible, or slow down

15. **B.** Stop and wait for a gap in the traffic

Sharing the road exam 4

1. **What is the recommended following distance for a car traveling at 60 miles per hour?**

   A. ▢ 6 seconds

   B. ▢ 8 seconds

   C. ▢ 10 seconds

   D. ▢ 12 seconds

2. **Who has the right of way when two vehicles arrive at a four-way stop at the same time?**

   A. ▢ The vehicle on the right

   B. ▢ The vehicle going straight

   C. ▢ The vehicle turning left

   D. ▢ The vehicle with the loudest horn

3. **When passing a bicycle on the road, what is the minimum passing distance required by law?**

   A. ▢ 3 feet

   B. ▢ 4 feet

   C. ▢ 5 feet

   D. ▢ 6 feet

4. **If you approach a pedestrian crossing the road, what should you do?**

   A. ▢ Honk your horn

   B. ▢ Speed up to pass quickly

   C. ▢ Slow down and allow the pedestrian to cross

   D. ▢ Swerve into the other lane to avoid the pedestrian

5. **What should you do when approaching a roundabout?**

A. ▫ Yield to all vehicles already in the roundabout

B. ▫ Speed up to beat other vehicles

C. ▫ Honk your horn loudly

D. ▫ Use the center lane to pass through quickly

6. **What should you do when approaching a school bus that is stopped with flashing red lights?**

A. ▫ Stop behind the bus

B. ▫ Pass the bus on the right

C. ▫ Slow down and proceed with caution

D. ▫ Speed up and pass quickly

7. **What should you do when approaching a funeral procession?**

A. ▫ Honk your horn loudly

B. ▫ Speed up to get around the procession

C. ▫ Slow down and proceed with caution

D. ▫ Pull over to the side of the road

8. **What should you do when approaching an intersection with a flashing yellow light?**

A. ▫ Stop and wait for the light to turn green

B. ▫ Slow down and proceed with caution

C. ▫ Speed up and pass quickly

D. ▫ Honk your horn loudly

9. **What should you do when approaching a road that is flooded with water?**

A. ▫ Drive through the water as fast as possibleDrive through the water as fast as possible

B. ▢ Pull over to the side of the road and wait

C. ▢ Slow down and proceed with caution

D. ▢ Drive through the water at the same speed as normal

10. How should you merge onto a highway?

A. ▢ Slow down and stop on the shoulder before merging

B. ▢ Speed up and force your way into traffic

C. ▢ Yield to vehicles already on the highway and merge when it is safe

D. ▢ Cut off other drivers to merge into a gap

11. What should you do when a pedestrian is crossing in a marked crosswalk?

A. ▢ Speed up to get past the pedestrian quickly

B. ▢ Stop behind the crosswalk and wait for the pedestrian to finish crossing

C. ▢ Drive around the pedestrian using the opposite lane

D. ▢ Stop at the crosswalk and yield to the pedestrian

12. What is the correct speed limit in a school zone when children are present?

A. ▢ 35 mph

B. ▢ 45 mph

C. ▢ 55 mph

D. ▢ 25 mph

13. What should you do when you approach a roundabout?

A. ▢ Drive straight through without slowing down

B. ▢ Stop at the entrance of the roundabout

C. ▢ Yield to vehicles already in the roundabout

D. ▢ Honk your horn to signal other drivers

14. What should you do when you approach a roundabout?

A. ▢ Drive straight through without slowing down

B. ▢ Stop at the entrance of the roundabout

C. ▢ Yield to vehicles already in the roundabout

D. ▢ Honk your horn to signal other drivers

15. When should you use your turn signals?

A. ▢ Only when other drivers are around

B. ▢ Only when you are about to turn

C. ▢ Only when changing lanes

D. ▢ Any time you are about to change direction on the road

Correct answers for sharing the road exam 4

1. **C.** 10 seconds
2. **A.** The vehicle on the right
3. **A.** 3 feet
4. **C.** Slow down and allow the pedestrian to cross
5. **A.** Yield to all vehicles already in the roundabout
6. **A.** Stop behind the bus
7. **D.** Pull over to the side of the road
8. **B.** Slow down and proceed with caution
9. **C.** Slow down and proceed with caution
10. **C.** Yield to vehicles already on the highway and merge when it is safe
11. **D.** Stop at the crosswalk and yield to the pedestrian
12. **D.** 25 mph
13. **C.** Yield to vehicles already in the roundabout
14. **D.** Any time you are about to change direction on the road
15. **A.** Slow down and be prepared to stop

Sharing the road exam 5

1. **What should you do when you approach an intersection with a stop sign?**

   A. ▢ Stop and proceed when all vehicles have cleared the intersection

   B. ▢ Yield to vehicles already in the intersection

   C. ▢ Drive through the intersection as quickly as possible

   D. ▢ Honk your horn to signal other drivers to get out of the way

2. **When driving in a construction zone, what should you do to ensure the safety of the workers?**

   A. ▢ Drive as close as possible to the construction workers

   B. ▢ Drive through the construction zone as quickly as possible

   C. ▢ Slow down and proceed with caution

   D. ▢ Honk your horn loudly

3. **When approaching a pedestrian who is crossing the road, what should you do?**

   A. ▢ Drive around the pedestrian

   B. ▢ Stop and wait for the pedestrian to cross

   C. ▢ Slow down and proceed with caution

   D. ▢ Honk your horn to scare the pedestrian

4. **What is the minimum following distance you should maintain when driving behind another vehicle on a highway?**

   A. ▢ Two car lengths

   B. ▢ One car length

   C. ▢ Three car lengths

   D. ▢ Four car lengths

5. **If a pedestrian is crossing the road in a crosswalk, what should a driver do?**

A. ▢ Stop and proceed when the pedestrian has passed

B. ▢ Slow down and proceed with caution

C. ▢ Drive faster to beat the pedestrian across

D. ▢ Honk the horn to scare the pedestrian

6. **When passing a bicycle on the road, what should a driver do to ensure the safety of the cyclist?**

A. ▢ Drive as close as possible to the bicycle

B. ▢ Pass the bicycle quickly

C. ▢ Wait until there is enough space and no oncoming traffic before passing

D. ▢ Honk the horn loudly

7. **When approaching a stopped emergency vehicle with its flashing lights activated, what should you do as a driver?**

A. ▢ Drive around the emergency vehicle

B. ▢ Stop and wait until the emergency vehicle moves

C. ▢ Slow down and proceed with caution

D. ▢ Speed up to get past the emergency vehicle as quickly as possible

8. **What should you do when you approach a roundabout?**

A. ▢ Stop and wait for all vehicles to clear the roundabout

B. ▢ Yield to vehicles already in the roundabout

C. ▢ Speed up to get through the roundabout as quickly as possible

D. ▢ Honk your horn to signal other drivers to get out of the way

9. **What should you do if you see a school bus with its red lights flashing and stop arm extended?**

A. ▫ Drive around the bus

B. ▫ Stop and wait until the bus drives off

C. ▫ Slow down and proceed with caution

D. ▫ Speed up to get past the bus as quickly as possible

10. When merging onto a highway, what should you do?

A. ▫ Stop and wait for all vehicles to clear the highway

B. ▫ Yield to vehicles already on the highway

C. ▫ Speed up to get on the highway as quickly as possible

D. ▫ Honk your horn to signal other drivers to get out of the way

11. When approaching a stopped train at a railroad crossing, what should you do?

A. ▫ Drive around the train

B. ▫ Stop and wait for the train to pass

C. ▫ Slow down and proceed with caution

D. ▫ Speed up to get past the train as quickly as possible

12. What is the minimum following distance you should maintain when driving behind another vehicle on a highway?

A. ▫ Two car lengths

B. ▫ One car length

C. ▫ Three car lengths

D. ▫ Four car lengths

13. If a pedestrian is crossing the road in a crosswalk, what should a driver do?

A. ▫ Stop and proceed when the pedestrian has passed

B. ▢ Slow down and proceed with caution

C. ▢ Drive faster to beat the pedestrian across

D. ▢ Honk the horn to scare the pedestrian

14. **When passing a bicycle on the road, what should a driver do to ensure the safety of the cyclist?**

A. ▢ Drive as close as possible to the bicycle

B. ▢ Pass the bicycle quickly

C. ▢ Wait until there is enough space and no oncoming traffic before passing

D. ▢ Honk the horn loudly

15. **When approaching a stopped emergency vehicle with its flashing lights activated, what should you do as a driver?**

A. ▢ Drive around the emergency vehicle

B. ▢ Stop and wait until the emergency vehicle moves

C. ▢ Slow down and proceed with caution

D. ▢ Speed up to get past the emergency vehicle as quickly as possible

Correct answers for sharing the road exam 5

1. **A.** Stop and proceed when all vehicles have cleared the intersection

2. **C.** Slow down and proceed with caution

3. **B.** Stop and wait for the pedestrian to cross

4. **C.** Three car lengths

5. **A.** Stop and proceed when the pedestrian has passed

6. **C.** Wait until there is enough space and no oncoming traffic before passing

7. **B.** Stop and wait until the emergency vehicle moves

8. **B.** Yield to vehicles already in the roundabout

9. **B.** Stop and wait until the bus drives off

10. **B.** Yield to vehicles already on the highway

11. **B.** Stop and wait for the train to pass

12. **C.** Three car lengths

13. **A.** Stop and proceed when the pedestrian has passed

14. **C.** Wait until there is enough space and no oncoming traffic before passing

15. **B.** Stop and wait until the emergency vehicle moves

Transportation of hazardous materials

Transportation of hazardous materials is a critical aspect of our daily lives as it involves the safe and efficient movement of dangerous goods from one place to another. These hazardous materials can range from toxic chemicals and flammable liquids to radioactive materials and biological substances. To ensure the safety of people and the environment, the transportation of hazardous materials is governed by strict regulations set by the United States Department of Transportation (USDOT) and the Ohio Department of Motor Vehicles (DMV).

In Ohio, those who operate commercial vehicles that transport hazardous materials are required to pass the Ohio DMV exam. The exam is designed to test the knowledge and understanding of the regulations, guidelines, and procedures related to the transportation of hazardous materials. It is essential for individuals to familiarize themselves with the regulations and guidelines set by the USDOT and Ohio DMV to ensure the safe and secure transportation of hazardous materials on the roads and highways of Ohio.

The Ohio DMV exam covers various topics, including the classification of hazardous materials, packaging and labeling requirements, transportation modes, security measures, and emergency response procedures. It is crucial for individuals to understand these topics to minimize the risk of accidents and spills during transportation.

In this chapter, we will delve into the transportation of hazardous materials in Ohio, exploring the regulations and guidelines set by the USDOT and Ohio DMV. We will also provide an overview of the topics covered in the Ohio DMV exam and the importance of compliance with the regulations to ensure the safety of people and the environment. By the end of this chapter, you will have a comprehensive understanding of the transportation of hazardous materials in Ohio and the importance of passing the Ohio DMV exam to transport hazardous materials safely and efficiently.

For training purposes, you can mark the ▢ symbol next to what you think is the correct answer: Once you have chosen the correct answer, use a pencil or pen to mark the ▢ symbol next to that answer.

Transportation of hazardous materials exam

1. **What is the main purpose of the regulations governing the transportation of hazardous materials in Ohio?**

   A. ▢ To ensure the safe and secure transportation of dangerous goods

   B. ▢ To promote the efficient movement of hazardous materials

   C. ▢ To generate revenue for the Ohio DMV

   D. ▢ To create employment opportunities for commercial drivers

2. **What is the first step in the transportation of hazardous materials in Ohio?**

   A. ▢ Loading the hazardous materials into the vehicle

   B. ▢ Securing the hazardous materials with appropriate restraints

   C. ▢ Properly classifying the hazardous materials

   D. ▢ Obtaining the necessary permits and certifications

3. **What are the requirements for labeling and packaging of hazardous materials in Ohio?**

   A. ▢ The labels must be legible and visible from all angles

   B. ▢ The packaging must be made of durable and resistant materials

   C. ▢ The labeling and packaging must comply with the USDOT

   D. ▢ All of the above

4. **What is the maximum weight limit for a commercial vehicle transporting hazardous materials in Ohio?**

   A. ▢ 80,000 pounds

   B. ▢ 75,000 pounds

   C. ▢ 90,000 pounds

D. ▫ 100,000 pounds

5. What is the role of the Ohio DMV in regulating the transportation of hazardous materials?

A. ▫ To issue permits and certifications

B. ▫ To enforce the regulations and guidelines

C. ▫ To provide training and education for commercial drivers

D. ▫ All of the above

6. What are the security measures required for commercial vehicles transporting hazardous materials in Ohio?

A. ▫ Properly locking the doors of the vehicle

B. ▫ Implementing a security plan to protect against theft or tampering

C. ▫ Conducting background checks on the commercial driver

D. ▫ All of the above

7. What is the procedure for responding to an accident involving a commercial vehicle transporting hazardous materials in Ohio?

A. ▫ Evacuate the area and call emergency services

B. ▫ Attempt to contain the spill

C. ▫ Inform the Ohio DMV of the accident

D. ▫ All of the above

8. What is the role of the commercial driver in the transportation of hazardous materials in Ohio?

A. ▫ To ensure the hazardous materials are properly classified

B. ▫ To comply with the regulations and guidelines set by the USDOT and Ohio DMV

C. ▫ To maintain the vehicle in a safe and secure condition

D. ▫ All of the above

9. **What is the penalty for non-compliance with the regulations governing the transportation of hazardous materials in Ohio?**

A. ▢ Fines and penalties imposed by the Ohio DMV

B. ▢ Criminal charges for environmental and safety violations

C. ▢ Loss of commercial driver's license

D. ▢ All of the above

10. **What is the importance of passing the Ohio DMV exam for commercial drivers transporting hazardous materials?**

A. ▢ To demonstrate knowledge and understanding of the regulations and guidelines

B. ▢ To ensure the safe and secure transportation of hazardous materials

C. ▢ To minimize the risk of accidents and spills

D. ▢ All of the above

11. **What type of materials are considered hazardous for the purposes of transportation in Ohio?**

A. ▢ Flammable liquids

B. ▢ Radioactive materials

C. ▢ Food and drinks

D. ▢ Clothing and textiles

12. **What are the requirements for training and certification of commercial drivers transporting hazardous materials in Ohio?**

A. ▢ Completion of a safety course and passing a written exam

B. ▢ Obtaining a commercial driver's license

C. ▢ Both A and B

D. ▢ Neither A nor B

13. What are the consequences of failing to properly label and package hazardous materials in Ohio?

A. ▢ Fines and penalties imposed by the Ohio DMV

B. ▢ Criminal charges for safety violations

C. ▢ Loss of commercial driver's license

D. ▢ All of the above

14. What is the minimum age requirement for a commercial driver transporting hazardous materials in Ohio?

A. ▢ 18 years

B. ▢ 21 years

C. ▢ 25 years

D. ▢ 30 years

15. What is the procedure for reporting a spill or release of hazardous materials during transportation in Ohio?

A. ▢ Report the incident to the Ohio DMV

B. ▢ Report the incident to emergency services

C. ▢ Report the incident to both the Ohio DMV and emergency services

D. ▢ None of the above

Correct answers for transportation of hazardous materials exam

1. **A.** To ensure the safe and secure transportation of dangerous goods

2. **C.** Properly classifying the hazardous materials

3. **D.** All of the above

4. **B.** 75,000 pounds

5. **D.** All of the above

6. **D.** All of the above

7. **D.** All of the above

8. **D.** All of the above

9. **D.** All of the above

10. **D.** All of the above

11. **A.** Flammable liquids

12. **C.** Both A and B

13. **D.** All of the above

14. **B.** 21 years

15. **C.** Report the incident to both the Ohio DMV and emergency services

Transportation of hazardous materials exam 2

1. What type of placards are required to be displayed on a commercial motor vehicle transporting hazardous materials?

   A. ▢ Orange

   B. ▢ Green

   C. ▢ Yellow

   D. ▢ Red

2. What is the minimum distance a commercial motor vehicle transporting hazardous materials must maintain from a flammable liquid storage facility?

   A. ▢ 100 feet

   B. ▢ 200 feet

   C. ▢ 300 feet

   D. ▢ 400 feet

3. What type of fire extinguisher is required to be carried on a commercial motor vehicle transporting hazardous materials?

   A. ▢ Class A

   B. ▢ Class B

   C. ▢ Class C

   D. ▢ Class D

4. What is the maximum amount of a hazardous material that a person can offer for transportation in a single package without being subject to federal hazard communication requirements?

   A. ▢ 5 gallons

   B. ▢ 10 gallons

C. ▢ 15 gallons

D. ▢ 25 gallons

5. **What type of documentation is required to be in the possession of the driver of a commercial motor vehicle transporting hazardous materials?**

   A. ▢ Bill of Lading

   B. ▢ Material Safety Data Sheet

   C. ▢ Shipping Papers

   D. ▢ All of the above

6. **What is the purpose of the Hazardous Materials Transportation Act (HMTA)?**

   A. ▢ To regulate the transportation of hazardous materials in order to protect the environment

   B. ▢ To regulate the transportation of hazardous materials in order to protect public health and safety

   C. ▢ To regulate the transportation of hazardous materials in order to protect the economy

   D. ▢ To regulate the transportation of hazardous materials in order to protect national security

7. **What is the definition of a hazardous material according to the HMTA?**

   A. ▢ Any substance that is potentially dangerous or harmful to human health or the environment

   B. ▢ Any substance that is flammable or explosive

   C. ▢ Any substance that is radioactive

   D. ▢ Any substance that is toxic or corrosive

8. **What is the requirement for a person or company transporting hazardous materials in Ohio?**

   A. ▢ They must have a permit from the Ohio Department of Transportation

   B. ▢ They must have a license from the Ohio Environmental Protection Agency

   C. ▢ They must have a certificate of training from an approved training provider

   D. ▢ They must have insurance coverage for liability and damages

9. **What is the proper way to label a hazardous material container according to HMTA regulations?**

   A. ▢ The label must be yellow with black lettering and must include the proper shipping name, identification number, and symbols

   B. ▢ The label must be green with white lettering and must include the proper shipping name, identification number, and symbols

   C. ▢ The label must be red with white lettering and must include the proper shipping name, identification number, and symbols

   D. ▢ The label must be blue with black lettering and must include the proper shipping name, identification number, and symbols

10. **What is the penalty for violating the HMTA regulations in Ohio?**

   A. ▢ A fine of up to $25,000

   B. ▢ A fine of up to $50,000

   C. ▢ A fine of up to $100,000

   D. ▢ Imprisonment of up to 5 years

11. **What is the minimum distance a vehicle carrying hazardous materials must maintain from the vehicle ahead?**

   A. ▢ To regulate the transportation of hazardous materials in order to protect the environment

   B. ▢ To regulate the transportation of hazardous materials in order to protect public health and safety

   C. ▢ To regulate the transportation of hazardous materials in order to protect the economy

   D. ▢ To regulate the transportation of hazardous materials in order to protect national security

12. **What is the definition of a hazardous material according to the HMTA?**

   A. ▢ Any substance that is potentially dangerous or harmful to human health or the environment

   B. ▢ Any substance that is flammable or explosive

   C. ▢ Any substance that is radioactive

   D. ▢ Any substance that is toxic or corrosive

13. **Which of the following is not required on the exterior of a vehicle transporting hazardous materials in Ohio?**

   A. ▢ Placards

   B. ▢ Shipping papers

   C. ▢ Emergency response information

   D. ▢ Special lighting equipment

14. **When driving a vehicle carrying hazardous materials, how often must you check the security of the load?**

   A. ▢ Every hour

   B. ▢ Every two hours

   C. ▢ Every three hours

   D. ▢ Every four hours

15. **What is the penalty for violating the HMTA regulations in Ohio?**

   A. ▢ A fine of up to $25,000

   B. ▢ A fine of up to $50,000

   C. ▢ A fine of up to $100,000

   D. ▢ Imprisonment of up to 5 years

Correct answers for transportation of hazardous materials exam 2

1. **D.** Red

2. **C.** 300 feet

3. **B.** Class B

4. **D.** 25 Gallons

5. **D.** All of the above

6. **B.** To regulate the transportation of hazardous materials in order to protect public health and safety

7. **A.** Any substance that is potentially dangerous or harmful to human health or the environment

8. **C.** They must have a certificate of training from an approved training provider

9. **A.** The label must be yellow with black lettering and must include the proper shipping name, identification number, and symbols

10. **B.** A fine of up to $50,000

11. **B.** To regulate the transportation of hazardous materials in order to protect public health and safety

12. **A.** Any substance that is potentially dangerous or harmful to human health or the environment

13. **D.** Special lighting equipment

14. **A.** Every hour

15. **B.** A fine of up to $50,000

Transportation of hazardous materials exam 3

1. **What should you do if there is a release of hazardous materials while transporting it?**

A. ▫ Continue driving to the destination

B. ▫ Pull over and evacuate the vehicle

C. ▫ Cover the spill with a cloth

D. ▫ Ignore it and hope it will go away

2. **What is the maximum speed limit for a vehicle carrying hazardous materials on a highway?**

A. ▫ 50 mph

B. ▫ 55 mph

C. ▫ 60 mph

D. ▫ 65 mph

3. **What type of placard must be displayed on the vehicle if it is carrying hazardous materials in a quantity that requires a placard?**

A. ▫ A diamond-shaped placard

B. ▫ A square-shaped placard

C. ▫ A circular-shaped placard

D. ▫ A triangular-shaped placard

4. **How many diamond-shaped hazardous material placards are required to be displayed on a vehicle carrying hazardous materials?**

A. ▫ 1

B. ▫ 2

C. ▫ 3

D. ☐ 4

5. **What type of marking is required on the packaging of hazardous materials being transported?**

A. ☐ A red stripe

B. ☐ A yellow stripe

C. ☐ A green stripe

D. ☐ A blue stripe

6. **What should you do if there is a release of hazardous materials while transporting it?**

A. ☐ Continue driving to the destination

B. ☐ Pull over and evacuate the vehicle

C. ☐ Cover the spill with a cloth

D. ☐ Ignore it and hope it will go away

7. **When driving a vehicle carrying hazardous materials, what is the maximum weight of a single package or container that can be placed on the top of the load?**

A. ☐ 50 pounds

B. ☐ 75 pounds

C. ☐ 100 pounds

D. ☐ 125 pounds

8. **What is the minimum distance a vehicle carrying hazardous materials must maintain from the vehicle ahead?**

A. ☐ 100 feet

B. ☐ 200 feet

C. ☐ 300 feet

D. ☐ 400 feet

9. **What should you do if there is a release of hazardous materials while transporting it?**

A. ▢ Continue driving to the destination

B. ▢ Pull over and evacuate the vehicle

C. ▢ Cover the spill with a cloth

D. ▢ Ignore it and hope it will go away

10. **What must be done if a package containing hazardous materials leaks while in transit?**

A. ▢ The driver must immediately evacuate the vehicle

B. ▢ The driver must immediately contain the leak

C. ▢ The driver must immediately secure the vehicle

D. ▢ The driver must immediately notify the authorities

11. **What type of training must a driver of a vehicle transporting hazardous materials receive?**

A. ▢ Basic safety training

B. ▢ Hazardous material handling training

C. ▢ Hazardous material transportation training

D. ▢ All of the above

12. **What is the maximum amount of hazardous material that can be transported in a single container?**

A. ▢ 55 gallons

B. ▢ 60 gallons

C. ▢ 110 gallons

D. ▢ 120 gallons

13. **What is the minimum age for a person to drive a vehicle transporting hazardous materials?**

A. ▢ 21 years

B. ▢ 18 years

C. ▢ 25 years

D. ▢ 30 years

14. When must a driver of a vehicle transporting hazardous materials notify the state and local emergency response agencies of the shipment?

A. ▢ Before entering the state

B. ▢ Before entering the city limits

C. ▢ Before entering a densely populated area

D. ▢ Before entering the county

15. What is the maximum number of hazardous material placards required to be displayed on a transport vehicle?

A. ▢ One

B. ▢ Two

C. ▢ Three

D. ▢ Four

Correct answers for transportation of hazardous materials exam 3

1. **B.** Pull over and evacuate the vehicle
2. **B.** 55 mph
3. **A.** A diamond-shaped placard
4. **A.** 1
5. **B.** A yellow stripe
6. **B.** Pull over and evacuate the vehicle
7. **C.** 100 pounds
8. **B.** 200 feet
9. **B.** Pull over and evacuate the vehicle
10. **D.** The driver must immediately notify the authorities
11. **D.** All of the above
12. **A.** 55 gallons
13. **A.** 21 years
14. **C.** Before entering a densely populated area
15. **A.** One

Transportation of hazardous materials exam 4

1. **Which of the following is required to transport hazardous materials in Ohio?**

   A. ▢ A driver's license

   B. ▢ A hazardous materials endorsement

   C. ▢ A commercial driver's license (CDL)

   D. ▢ A valid state ID

2. **When transporting hazardous materials, what is the maximum speed limit for vehicles in Ohio?**

   A. ▢ 55 mph

   B. ▢ 65 mph

   C. ▢ 70 mph

   D. ▢ 75 mph

3. **What is the minimum age requirement to obtain a hazardous materials endorsement in Ohio?**

   A. ▢ 16 years old

   B. ▢ 8 years old

   C. ▢ 21 years old

   D. ▢ 25 years old

4. **When transporting hazardous materials, what is required to be displayed on the vehicle?**

   A. ▢ The driver's name

   B. ▢ The vehicle's make and model

   C. ▢ The hazardous materials placard

   D. ▢ The shipping manifest

5. Which of the following is NOT a class of hazardous materials?

A. ▢ Class 1: Explosives

B. ▢ Class 2: Gases

C. ▢ Class 3: Flammable liquids

D. ▢ Class 5: Miscellaneous dangerous goods

6. If a hazardous materials spill occurs during transportation, what should the driver do first?

A. ▢ Report the spill to the local police department

B. ▢ Evacuate the area immediately

C. ▢ Try to contain the spill, if possible

D. ▢ Call the company's customer service line

7. Which of the following is NOT a type of hazmat container?

A. ▢ Drums

B. ▢ Cylinders

C. ▢ Bulk packaging

D. ▢ Glass bottles

8. How often must hazardous materials training be completed by drivers in Ohio?

A. ▢ Every year

B. ▢ Every two years

C. ▢ Every three years

D. ▢ Every five years

9. What is the maximum weight allowed for a single package of hazardous materials transported on Ohio highways?

A. ▢ 50 pounds

B. ▢ 100 pounds

C. ▢ 150 pounds

D. ▢ 200 pounds

10. **When transporting hazardous materials, what is the minimum required amount of fire extinguishers for a vehicle?**

A. ▢ One 5-pound extinguisher

B. ▢ Two 10-pound extinguishers

C. ▢ Two 5-pound extinguishers

D. ▢ One 10-pound extinguisher

11. **Which of the following is a requirement for a hazmat driver in Ohio?**

A. ▢ A minimum of three years of driving experience

B. ▢ No history of traffic violations or accidents

C. ▢ Passing a background check and fingerprinting

D. ▢ A high school diploma or equivalent

12. **Which of the following is NOT an acceptable hazmat label for packages?**

A. ▢ Limited Quantity

B. ▢ ORM-D

C. ▢ Class 6

D. ▢ Explosive

13. **What is the emergency phone number that must be displayed on a hazmat vehicle in Ohio?**

A. ▢ 911

B. ▢ 511

C. ▢ 811

D. ▢ 711

14. Which of the following documents is required to be carried by a hazmat driver in Ohio?

A. ▢ Vehicle registration

B. ▢ Insurance card

C. ▢ Shipping papers

D. ▢ Driver's license

15. What is the maximum amount of time a hazmat driver can spend behind the wheel before taking a break in Ohio?

A. ▢ 2 hours

B. ▢ 3 hours

C. ▢ 4 hours

D. ▢ 5 hours

Correct answers for transportation of hazardous materials exam 4

1. **B.** A hazardous materials endorsement
2. **A.** 55 mph
3. **B.** 18 years old
4. **C.** The hazardous materials placard
5. **D.** Class 5: Miscellaneous dangerous goods
6. **B.** Evacuate the area immediately
7. **D.** Glass bottles
8. **B.** Every two years
9. **C.** 150 pounds
10. **B.** Two 10-pound extinguishers
11. **C.** Passing a background check and fingerprinting
12. **C.** Class 6
13. **A.** 911
14. **C.** Shipping papers
15. **B.** 3 hours

Transportation of hazardous materials exam 5

1. When transporting hazardous materials, what is the minimum amount of space required between the driver and the cargo area in a hazmat vehicle?

   A. ▢ 25 feet

   B. ▢ 50 feet

   C. ▢ 75 feet

   D. ▢ 100 feet

2. Which of the following is a type of hazmat endorsement in Ohio?

   A. ▢ H

   B. ▢ P

   C. ▢ X

   D. ▢ Z

3. Which of the following is NOT a required component of a hazmat security plan in Ohio?

   A. ▢ A driver safety checklist

   B. ▢ Background checks for employees with access to hazmat materials

   C. ▢ A communication plan

   D. ▢ A training program for employees involved in hazmat transportation

4. Which of the following is a requirement for a hazmat vehicle in Ohio?

   A. ▢ A reflective safety vest for the driver

   B. ▢ A backup camera

   C. ▢ A first-aid kit

   D. ▢ A fire suppression syste

5. Which of the following is a type of placard that must be displayed on a hazmat vehicle in Ohio?

A. ▢ Corrosive

B. ▢ Infectious

C. ▢ Flammable

D. ▢ All of the above

6. What is the maximum penalty for violating Ohio's hazmat transportation regulations?

A. ▢ $1,000 fine

B. ▢ $10,000 fine

C. ▢ $25,000 fine

D. ▢ $50,000 fine

7. Which of the following is a required item in a hazmat emergency response kit in Ohio?

A. ▢ Shovel

B. ▢ Flashlight

C. ▢ Crowbar

D. ▢ Ax

8. Which of the following is NOT a requirement for a hazmat endorsement on a CDL in Ohio?

A. ▢ Passing a written test

B. ▢ Passing a driving test

C. ▢ Completing a hazmat training course

D. ▢ Obtaining a medical certificate

9. Which of the following is a requirement for a hazmat vehicle in Ohio?

A. ▢ A reflective safety vest for the driver

B. ▢ A backup camera

C. ▢ A first-aid kit

D. ▢ A fire suppression system

10. What is the maximum allowed speed for a vehicle transporting hazardous materials in Ohio?

A. ▢ 35 mph

B. ▢ 45 mph

C. ▢ 55 mph

D. ▢ 65 mph

11. Which of the following is a required placard for a vehicle transporting certain types of hazardous materials in Ohio?

A. ▢ Flammable Gas

B. ▢ Organic Peroxide

C. ▢ Oxidizer

D. ▢ All of the above

12. What is the minimum age requirement for a driver to obtain a hazmat endorsement on their CDL in Ohio?

A. ▢ 18 years old

B. ▢ 21 years old

C. ▢ 25 years old

D. ▢ 30 years old

13. Which of the following is a requirement for a hazmat driver's vehicle inspection in Ohio?

A. ▢ Checking the tire pressure

B. □ Testing the brakes

C. □ Inspecting the radio

D. □ Cleaning the windows

14. **Which of the following is a type of hazardous material that requires a special permit for transportation in Ohio?**

A. □ Gasoline

B. □ Oxygen

C. □ Radioactive material

D. □ Sulfuric acid

15. **Which of the following is a requirement for a hazmat driver's security plan in Ohio?**

A. □ A detailed map of the driver's route

B. □ A list of emergency contacts

C. □ A description of the driver's vehicle

D. □ A copy of the driver's insurance policy

Correct answers for transportation of hazardous materials exam 5

1. **B.** 50 feet
2. **A.** H
3. **A.** A driver safety checklist
4. **D.** A fire suppression system
5. **D.** All of the above
6. **C.** $25,000 fine
7. **B.** Flashlight
8. **B.** Passing a driving test
9. **D.** A fire suppression system
10. **C.** 55 mph
11. **D.** All of the above
12. **B.** 21 years old
13. **C.** Inspecting the radio
14. **C.** Radioactive material
15. **B.** A list of emergency contacts

Vehicle registration and insurance

Vehicle registration and insurance are essential components of owning and operating a car in Ohio. Not only are they legally required, but they also provide important protections for both drivers and other individuals on the road. The Ohio Department of Motor Vehicles (DMV) requires all vehicle owners to register their cars and obtain insurance coverage before hitting the road.

Vehicle registration in Ohio involves several steps, including providing proof of ownership, providing identification, and paying registration fees. Vehicle owners must also provide proof of insurance coverage when registering their cars. Failure to register a vehicle can result in fines and legal consequences, including the impoundment of the car.

Ohio also requires that all vehicle owners carry minimum insurance coverage to protect themselves and others in the event of an accident. The minimum required coverage includes liability insurance, which covers damages and injuries to other drivers and their property. Vehicle owners may choose to obtain additional coverage, such as collision and comprehensive insurance, to protect against damage to their own cars.

When obtaining insurance coverage in Ohio, vehicle owners should shop around to find the best policy for their needs and budget. Factors such as the age and make of the car, driving history, and personal circumstances can all impact insurance rates. It is also important to understand the different types of coverage and the limitations of each policy.

The Ohio DMV exam includes questions related to vehicle registration and insurance, so it is important for drivers to understand these requirements and laws. Knowing how to register a car, obtain insurance coverage, and maintain compliance with state regulations can help drivers stay safe on the road and avoid legal consequences. By understanding the importance of vehicle registration and insurance, drivers can protect themselves and others and enjoy the freedom and convenience of owning a car in Ohio.

For training purposes, you can mark the ▢ symbol next to what you think is the correct answer: Once you have chosen the correct answer, use a pencil or pen to mark the ▢ symbol next to that answer.

So let's get started!

Vehicle registration and insurance exam

1. **What is the minimum amount of uninsured motorist coverage required in Ohio?**

   A. ▢ $10,000 per person, $20,000 per accident

   B. ▢ $25,000 per person, $50,000 per accident

   C. ▢ $50,000 per person, $100,000 per accident

   D. ▢ $100,000 per person, $300,000 per accident

2. **What is the penalty for driving without a valid driver's license in Ohio?**

   A. ▢ $50 fine

   B. ▢ $100 fine

   C. ▢ License suspension

   D. ▢ All of the above

3. **How often do Ohio vehicle owners need to renew their license plates?**

   A. ▢ Annually

   B. ▢ Bi-annually

   C. ▢ Tri-annually

   D. ▢ Quadrennially

4. **Which of the following must be presented to renew vehicle registration in Ohio?**

   A. ▢ Valid driver's license

   B. ▢ Proof of insurance

   C. ▢ Emissions testing certification

   D. ▢ All of the above

5. **What is the minimum amount of property damage liability coverage required in Ohio?**

A. ▢ $5,000

B. ▢ $10,000

C. ▢ $25,000

D. ▢ $50,000

6. **What type of vehicle requires an Ohio Commercial Driver's License (CDL)?**

A. ▢ Vehicles weighing 10,001 pounds or more

B. ▢ Vehicles designed to transport 16 or more passengers

C. ▢ Vehicles transporting hazardous materials

D. ▢ All of the above

7. **What is the minimum amount of personal injury protection (PIP) coverage required in Ohio?**

A. ▢ $10,000

B. ▢ $25,000

C. ▢ $50,000

D. ▢ PIP coverage is not required in Ohio

8. **Which of the following factors can affect your auto insurance premiums in Ohio?**

A. ▢ Age and gender

B. ▢ Marital status

C. ▢ Driving record

D. ▢ All of the above

9. **What is the maximum speed limit for school zones in Ohio?**

A. ▢ 15 mph

B. ▢ 20 mph

C. ▢ 25 mph

D. ▢ 30 mph

10. **What type of insurance coverage will pay for damages to your vehicle if you are in an accident with an uninsured driver?**

A. ▢ Collision coverage

B. ▢ Comprehensive coverage

C. ▢ Liability coverage

D. ▢ Uninsured motorist coverage

11. **What is the maximum speed limit for a passenger car on a rural freeway in Ohio?**

A. ▢ 55 mph

B. ▢ 65 mph

C. ▢ 70 mph

D. ▢ 75 mph

12. **What is the minimum amount of bodily injury liability coverage required for a driver of a commercial motor vehicle in Ohio?**

A. ▢ $15,000 per person, $30,000 per accident

B. ▢ $25,000 per person, $50,000 per accident

C. ▢ $50,000 per person, $100,000 per accident

D. ▢ $100,000 per person, $300,000 per accident

13. **Which of the following documents must be carried in a vehicle at all times in Ohio?**

A. ▢ Driver's license

B. ▢ Vehicle registration

C. ▢ Proof of insurance

D. ▢ All of the above

14. Which of the following factors can affect your auto insurance premiums in Ohio?

A. ▢ Vehicle make and model

B. ▢ Driving location

C. ▢ Annual mileage

D. ▢ All of the above

15. What is the penalty for driving without insurance in Ohio?

A. ▢ $50 fine

B. ▢ $100 fine

C. ▢ License suspension

D. ▢ All of the above

Correct answers for vehicle registration and insurance exam

1. **A.** $10,000 per person, $20,000 per accident
2. **D.** All of the above
3. **A.** Annually
4. **D.** All of the above
5. **A.** $5,000
6. **D.** All of the above
7. **D.** PIP coverage is not required in Ohio
8. **D.** All of the above
9. **A.** 15 mph
10. **D.** Uninsured motorist coverage
11. **D.** 75 mph
12. **D.** $100,000 per person, $300,000 per accident
13. **D.** All of the above
14. **D.** All of the above
15. **D.** All of the above

Vehicle registration and insurance exam 2

1. What type of insurance coverage will pay for damages to your own vehicle if you are in an accident that is your fault?

    A. ▫ Liability coverage

    B. ▫ Collision coverage

    C. ▫ Comprehensive coverage

    D. ▫ Uninsured motorist coverage

2. What is the minimum amount of property damage liability coverage required in Ohio?

    A. ▫ $10,000

    B. ▫ $25,000

    C. ▫ $50,000

    D. ▫ $100,000

3. What is the maximum speed limit for a truck or other commercial motor vehicle on a rural interstate in Ohio?

    A. ▫ 55 mph

    B. ▫ 65 mph

    C. ▫ 70 mph

    D. ▫ 75 mph

4. Which of the following vehicles requires an Ohio motorcycle endorsement on your driver's license?

    A. ▫ A motor scooter with an engine smaller than 50cc

    B. ▫ A motorized bicycle with pedals

    C. ▫ A motorcycle with an engine larger than 250cc

D. ▢ A moped with an engine larger than 50cc

5. What type of insurance coverage will pay for damages to your vehicle if you hit an animal on the road?

A. ▢ Collision coverage

B. ▢ Comprehensive coverage

C. ▢ Liability coverage

D. ▢ Uninsured motorist coverage

6. How many days do you have to register a newly purchased vehicle in Ohio?

A. ▢ 5 days

B. ▢ 10 days

C. ▢ 15 days

D. ▢ 30 days

7. What is the maximum speed limit for a truck or other commercial motor vehicle on an urban interstate in Ohio?

A. ▢ 50 mph

B. ▢ 55 mph

C. ▢ 60 mph

D. ▢ 65 mph

8. What type of insurance coverage will pay for damages to someone else's vehicle or property if you are in an accident that is your fault?

A. ▢ Liability coverage

B. ▢ Collision coverage

C. ▢ Comprehensive coverage

D. ▢ Uninsured motorist coverage

9. Which of the following is not a factor that can affect your auto insurance premiums in Ohio?

A. ▢ Gender

B. ▢ Age

C. ▢ Marital status

D. ▢ Vehicle color

10. What is the minimum amount of uninsured motorist coverage required in Ohio?

A. ▢ $15,000 per person/$30,000 per accident

B. ▢ $25,000 per person/$50,000 per accident

C. ▢ $50,000 per person/$100,000 per accident

D. ▢ $100,000 per person/$300,000 per accident

11. What type of insurance coverage will pay for damages to your vehicle if it is stolen or damaged by something other than a collision?

A. ▢ Liability coverage

B. ▢ Collision coverage

C. ▢ Comprehensive coverage

D. ▢ Uninsured motorist coverage

12. Which of the following documents is needed to register a vehicle in Ohio?

A. ▢ Proof of insurance

B. ▢ Vehicle registration certificate

C. ▢ Vehicle title

D. ▢ Driver's license

13. Which of the following factors can affect your auto insurance premiums in Ohio?

A. ▢ Driving record

B. ▢ Vehicle make and model

C. ▢ Age and gender

D. ▢ All of the above

14. Which of the following is not required to register a vehicle in Ohio?

A. ▢ Vehicle inspection report

B. ▢ Proof of insurance

C. ▢ Driver's license

D. ▢ Payment of registration fees

15. If you fail to provide proof of insurance during a traffic stop, what may happen to your vehicle registration?

A. ▢ It may be suspended

B. ▢ It may be canceled

C. ▢ It may be revoked

D. ▢ It may be terminated

Correct answers for vehicle registration and insurance exam 2

1. **B.** Collision coverage

2. **A.** $10,000

3. **C.** 70 mph

4. **C.** A motorcycle with an engine larger than 250cc

5. **B.** Comprehensive coverage

6. **D.** 30 days

7. **D.** 65 mph

8. **A.** Liability coverage

9. **D.** Vehicle color

10. **B.** $25,000 per person/$50,000 per accident

11. **C.** Comprehensive coverage

12. **C.** Vehicle title

13. **D.** All of the above

14. **A.** Vehicle inspection report

15. **A.** It may be suspended

Vehicle registration and insurance exam 3

1. **Which of the following is a common type of insurance coverage for personal vehicles?**

   A. ▢ Liability insurance

   B. ▢ Homeowners insurance

   C. ▢ Life insurance

   D. ▢ Health insurance

2. **What does the acronym "VIN" stand for in the context of vehicle registration and insurance?**

   A. ▢ Vehicle Identification Number

   B. ▢ Vehicle Insurance Number

   C. ▢ Vehicle Inspection Number

   D. ▢ Vehicle Import Number

3. **Which of the following is a requirement for registering a vehicle in most jurisdictions?**

   A. ▢ Proof of insurance

   B. ▢ Driver's license

   C. ▢ Social security card

   D. ▢ Birth certificate

4. **What does "collision coverage" typically cover in vehicle insurance?**

   A. ▢ Damage caused by natural disasters

   B. ▢ Damage caused by theft or vandalism

   C. ▢ Damage caused by collisions with other vehicles

   D. ▢ Medical expenses for the driver and passengers

5. **Which of the following is a type of insurance coverage that can help pay for medical expenses and lost wages after a car accident?**

   A. ▫ Liability insurance

   B. ▫ Collision insurance

   C. ▫ Comprehensive insurance

   D. ▫ Personal injury protection (PIP)

6. **Which of the following factors can affect the cost of auto insurance premiums?**

   A. ▫ Age of the vehicle

   B. ▫ Color of the vehicle

   C. ▫ Number of airbags in the vehicle

   D. ▫ Age and driving record of the driver

7. **What is the purpose of an emissions test in vehicle registration?**

   A. ▫ To ensure the vehicle is roadworthy

   B. ▫ To check the v ehicle's fuel efficiency

   C. ▫ To measure the vehicle's exhaust emissions

   D. ▫ To evaluate the vehicle's overall safety

8. **What does "deductible" refer to in the context of vehicle insurance?**

   A. ▫ The amount of money the insurance company will pay in case of a claim

   B. ▫ The amount of money the policyholder must pay out of pocket before insurance coverage kicks in

   C. ▫ The length of time the policyholder has to wait before making a claim

   D. ▫ The total amount of coverage provided by the insurance policy

9. **What is the purpose of liability insurance in vehicle registration and insurance?**

A. ▢ To protect the driver against theft or vandalism

B. ▢ To cover medical expenses for the driver and passengers

C. ▢ To pay for damages caused by the driver to other people or their property

D. ▢ To provide coverage for collisions with other vehicles

10. What does "comprehensive coverage" typically cover in vehicle insurance?

A. ▢ Damage caused by natural disasters

B. ▢ Damage caused by theft or vandalism

C. ▢ Damage caused by collisions with other vehicles

D. ▢ Medical expenses for the driver and passengers

11. What is the minimum age requirement for most jurisdictions to register and drive a car?

A. ▢ 16 years old

B. ▢ 18 years old

C. ▢ 21 years old

D. ▢ 25 years old

12. Which of the following is a requirement for renewing vehicle registration in most jurisdictions?

A. ▢ Proof of insurance

B. ▢ Driver's license

C. ▢ Vehicle inspection

D. ▢ Proof of ownership

13. Which of the following is a type of coverage that can help pay for damages caused by an uninsured driver?

A. ▢ Collision insurance

B. ▢ Liability insurance

C. ▢ Comprehensive insurance

D. ▢ Uninsured motorist coverage

14. Which of the following factors can affect the cost of auto insurance premiums?

A. ▢ Color of the vehicle

B. ▢ Number of cup holders in the vehicle

C. ▢ Age and driving record of the driver

D. ▢ Number of passengers the vehicle can carry

15. What does "rebuilt title" mean in the context of vehicle registration and insurance?

A. ▢ The vehicle was previously salvaged and has since been repaired

B. ▢ The vehicle was previously stolen and has since been recovered

C. ▢ The vehicle was previously used by a rental car company

D. ▢ The vehicle was previously owned by a celebrity or public figure

Correct answers for vehicle registration and insurance exam 3

1. **A.** Liability insurance

2. **A.** Vehicle Identification Number

3. **A.** Proof of insurance

4. **C.** Damage caused by collisions with other vehicles

5. **D.** Personal injury protection (PIP)

6. **D.** Age and driving record of the driver

7. **C.** To measure the vehicle's exhaust emissions

8. **B.** The amount of money the policyholder must pay out of pocket before insurance coverage kicks in.

9. **C.** To pay for damages caused by the driver to other people or their property.

10. **A.** Damage caused by natural disasters.

11. **B.** 18 years old.

12. **A.** Proof of insurance.

13. **D.** Uninsured motorist coverage.

14. **C.** Age and driving record of the driver.

15. **A.** The vehicle was previously salvaged and has since been repaired.

Vehicle registration and insurance exam 4

1. **What is the penalty for driving without insurance in Ohio?**

   A. ▢ A fine of up to $1,000

   B. ▢ A fine of up to $500 and a 6-month license suspension

   C. ▢ A fine of up to $1,000 and a 1-year license suspension

   D. ▢ A fine of up to $500 and a 1-year license suspension

2. **How long do you have to register your out-of-state vehicle after moving to Ohio?**

   A. ▢ 15 days

   B. ▢ 30 days

   C. ▢ 60 days

   D. ▢ 60 days

3. **Which of the following documents is required to register a vehicle in Ohio?**

   A. ▢ Driver's license

   B. ▢ Insurance card

   C. ▢ Vehicle title

   D. ▢ All of the above

4. **What is the minimum amount of liability insurance coverage required for Ohio drivers?**

   A. ▢ $10,000 for property damage

   B. ▢ $25,000 for bodily injury or death of one person

   C. ▢ $50,000 for bodily injury or death of two or more people

   D. ▢ All of the above

5. **Which of the following factors can affect your Ohio car insurance rates?**

A. ▢ Age

B. ▢ Driving record

C. ▢ Driving record

D. ▢ All of the above

6. **What is the Ohio Bureau of Motor Vehicles (BMV) responsible for?**

A. ▢ Driver's licenses

B. ▢ Vehicle registrations

C. ▢ Issuing license plates

D. ▢ All of the above

7. **Which of the following is true regarding temporary license plates in Ohio?**

A. ▢ They are not required

B. ▢ They are valid for 30 days

C. ▢ They can only be obtained from a BMV office

D. ▢ They are valid for 60 days

8. **What is the maximum amount of time you have to renew your vehicle registration in Ohio before it expires?**

A. ▢ 15 days

B. ▢ 30 days

C. ▢ 45 days

D. ▢ 90 days

9. **Which of the following is required to obtain an Ohio driver's license?**

A. ▢ A social security card

B. ▢ Proof of residency

C. ▢ A written and driving test

D. ▢ All of the above

10. Which of the following is NOT a factor that affects your Ohio car insurance rates?

A. ▢ Your credit score

B. ▢ Your age

C. ▢ Your gender

D. ▢ Your driving record

11. What is the penalty for driving with an expired registration in Ohio?

A. ▢ $50 fine

B. ▢ $75 fine

C. ▢ $100 fine

D. ▢ $125 fine

12. How often are Ohio drivers required to have their vehicles undergo an emissions test?

A. ▢ Every year

B. ▢ Every other year

C. ▢ Every three years

D. ▢ Only if the vehicle is over 10 years old

13. What is the minimum amount of bodily injury liability insurance required for Ohio drivers?

A. ▢ $10,000 per person

B. ▢ $25,000 per person

C. ▢ $50,000 per accident

D. ▢ $100,000 per accident

14. Which of the following documents do you need to bring with you when registering a leased vehicle in Ohio?

A. ▢ Lease agreement

B. ▢ Power of attorney

C. ▢ Manufacturer's certificate of origin

D. ▢ Title certificate

15. What is the Ohio state law on cell phone use while driving?

A. ▢ All drivers are prohibited from using cell phones while driving

B. ▢ Only novice drivers are prohibited from using cell phones while driving

C. ▢ Only commercial drivers are prohibited from using cell phones while driving

D. ▢ There is no state law on cell phone use while driving

Correct answers for vehicle registration and insurance exam 4

1. **B.** A fine of up to $500 and a 6-month license suspension
2. **D.** 90 days
3. **D.** All of the above
4. **D.** All of the above
5. **D.** All of the above
6. **D.** All of the above
7. **B.** They are valid for 30 days
8. **D.** All of the above
9. **D.** All of the above
10. **C.** Your gender
11. **C.** $100 fine
12. **B.** Every other year
13. **B.** $25,000 per person
14. **A.** Lease agreement
15. **B.** Only novice drivers are prohibited from using cell phones while driving

Vehicle registration and insurance exam 5

1. **What is the minimum liability insurance coverage required for private passenger vehicles in Ohio?**

   A. ▫ $15,000 per person for bodily injury, $30,000 per accident for bodily injury, and $5,000 for property damage

   B. ▫ $25,000 per person for bodily injury, $50,000 per accident for bodily injury, and $25,000 for property damage.

   C. ▫ $30,000 per person for bodily injury, $60,000 per accident for bodily injury, and $10,000 for property damage

   D. ▫ $50,000 per person for bodily injury, $100,000 per accident for bodily injury, and $25,000 for property damage

2. **When must a driver in Ohio submit proof of financial responsibility, such as insurance coverage, to the Bureau of Motor Vehicles (BMV)?**

   A. ▫ Only when requested by a police officer

   B. ▫ When registering a vehicle or applying for a driver's license

   C. ▫ After being involved in an accident

   D. ▫ Only when driving outside of Ohio

3. **In Ohio, what is the maximum speed limit in a municipal corporation unless otherwise posted?**

   A. ▫ 25 miles per hour

   B. ▫ 35 miles per hour

   C. ▫ 45 miles per hour

   D. ▫ 55 miles per hour

4. **Which of the following is a requirement for an Ohio driver to legally transport a child in a car seat?**

A. ▢ The child must be at least 2 years old.

B. ▢ The car seat must be facing forward.

C. ▢ The car seat must be secured with the vehicle's safety belts.

D. ▢ The car seat must meet federal safety standards.

5. **In Ohio, when can a driver legally make a left turn on red?**

A. ▢ When turning from a one-way street onto another one-way street

B. ▢ When turning from a two-way street onto a one-way street

C. ▢ When turning from a two-way street onto another two-way street

D. ▢ Left turns on red are never allowed in Ohio

6. **Which of the following is a reason for the Bureau of Motor Vehicles (BMV) to suspend a driver's license in Ohio?**

A. ▢ Failure to pay a traffic ticket fine

B. ▢ A single speeding ticket

C. ▢ Failure to renew vehicle registration on time

D. ▢ Driving with an expired license plate sticker

7. **In Ohio, what is the maximum speed limit on interstate highways unless otherwise posted?**

A. ▢ 50 miles per hour

B. ▢ 60 miles per hour

C. ▢ 70 miles per hour

D. ▢ 80 miles per hour

8. **What is the minimum amount of medical payment coverage required for car insurance policies in Ohio?**

A. ▢ $5,000

B. □ $10,000

C. □ $15,000

D. □ Medical payment coverage is optional in Ohio.

9. **In Ohio, what is the minimum age for a child to ride in the front seat of a vehicle?**

A. □ 2 years old

B. □ 4 years old

C. □ 8 years old

D. □ There is no minimum age specified in Ohio law

10. **Which of the following is a reason for the BMV to require a driver to take a driver's license examination in Ohio?**

A. □ A change of address

B. □ A change of name

C. □ A suspension or revocation of a driver's license

D. □ All of the above

11. **In Ohio, what is the minimum amount of property damage liability coverage required for car insurance policies?**

A. □ $5,000

B. □ $10,000

C. □ $15,000

D. □ $25,000

12. **In most states, how long do you have to renew your vehicle registration before it expires?**

A. □ 15 days

B. □ 30 days

C. ▢ 60 days

D. ▢ 90 days

13. What type of auto insurance covers damage to your own car in the event of an accident?

A. ▢ Liability insurance

B. ▢ Collision insurance

C. ▢ Comprehensive insurance

D. ▢ Uninsured motorist insurance

14. In which of the following situations might an insurance company deny a claim?

A. ▢ The driver who caused the accident was uninsured

B. ▢ The driver was using the car for commercial purposes

C. ▢ The damage was caused by an act of nature

D. ▢ The driver had a valid driver's license

15. What does it mean if your car's title is branded as "salvage"?

A. ▢ The car has been stolen

B. ▢ The car was previously used as a rental vehicle

C. ▢ The car has been in a major accident and deemed a total loss by the insurance company

D. ▢ The car has a history of frequent breakdowns

Correct answers for vehicle registration and insurance exam 5

1. **B.** $25,000 per person for bodily injury, $50,000 per accident for bodily injury, and $25,000 for property damage.

2. **B.** When registering a vehicle or applying for a driver's license

3. **A.** 25 miles per hour

4. **D.** The car seat must meet federal safety standards.

5. **A.** When turning from a one-way street onto another one-way street

6. **A.** Failure to pay a traffic ticket fine

7. **C.** 70 miles per hour

8. **D.** Medical payment coverage is optional in Ohio.

9. **D.** There is no minimum age specified in Ohio law.

10. **D.** All of the above

11. **D.** $25,000

12. **B.** 30 days

13. **B.** Collision insurance

14. **B.** The driver was using the car for commercial purposes

15. **C.** The car has been in a major accident and deemed a total loss by the insurance company

Emergencies

When it comes to driving, emergencies can happen at any time and without warning. It's essential for drivers to be prepared for emergencies and know how to react in those situations. The Ohio DMV exam includes questions on emergency procedures, and it's important for drivers to understand these concepts in order to pass the exam and be prepared for the unexpected.

Emergencies can take many forms while driving, including accidents, mechanical failures, weather-related incidents, and medical emergencies. Knowing what to do in each of these situations can help prevent further harm and ensure the safety of all involved.

In Ohio, drivers are required to follow certain procedures in the event of an emergency. For example, if you are involved in an accident, you must stop your vehicle and remain at the scene until law enforcement arrives. If someone is injured, you must provide reasonable assistance, such as calling for medical help.

In addition to accidents, mechanical failures can also occur while driving. This can include flat tires, engine problems, or other issues that may cause a vehicle to become disabled. In these situations, it's important to move your vehicle out of traffic and turn on your hazard lights to warn other drivers.

Weather-related emergencies can also pose a significant threat to drivers. Ohio experiences a range of weather conditions, including snow, ice, and severe thunderstorms. Knowing how to adjust your driving to these conditions can help prevent accidents and keep you safe on the road.

Finally, medical emergencies can occur while driving. It's important to know how to recognize the signs of a medical emergency and what to do in those situations. This may involve pulling over to a safe location and calling for medical help.

Overall, emergencies can happen at any time while driving. Understanding the proper procedures and techniques for handling these situations is crucial for all drivers, and it's an important part of the Ohio DMV exam. By studying and practicing emergency procedures, you can be better prepared for any unexpected situations on the road.

For training purposes, you can mark the ▢ symbol next to what you think is the correct answer: Once you have chosen the correct answer, use a pencil or pen to mark the ▢ symbol next to that answer.

So, let's get started!

Emergencies exam

1. **What should you do if you are involved in an accident in Ohio?**

   A. ▢ Drive away from the scene as quickly as possible

   B. ▢ Call 911 and leave the scene of the accident

   C. ▢ Stop your vehicle and remain at the scene until law enforcement arrives

   D. ▢ Move your vehicle out of traffic and continue driving

2. **In Ohio, what should you do if you hear a continuous siren or horn from a police, fire, or other emergency vehicle?**

   A. ▢ Slow down and proceed with caution

   B. ▢ Speed up to get out of the way quickly

   C. ▢ Stop and pull over to the right side of the road

   D. ▢ Ignore it and continue driving

3. **What should you do if you encounter a severe thunderstorm while driving in Ohio?**

   A. ▢ Turn off your headlights and wait for the storm to pass

   B. ▢ Increase your speed to get through the storm more quickly

   C. ▢ Pull over to a safe location and wait for the storm to pass

   D. ▢ Continue driving as normal

4. **What should you do if you encounter black ice on the road in Ohio?**

   A. ▢ Slow down and brake gently

   B. ▢ Speed up to get through it more quickly

   C. ▢ Turn off your headlights to avoid glare

   D. ▢ Ignore it and continue driving normally

5. **What should you do if you suspect someone is having a heart attack while driving in Ohio?**

A. ▢ Continue driving to the nearest hospital

B. ▢ Pull over to a safe location and call for medical help

C. ▢ Ask the person if they need medical help and continue driving if they say no

D. ▢ Ignore the situation and continue driving as normal

6. **What should you do if your brakes fail while driving in Ohio?**

A. ▢ Slam on the brakes to see if they will start working again

B. ▢ Downshift to a lower gear and use the emergency brake to slow down

C. ▢ Continue driving as normal

D. ▢ Turn off the engine to slow down

7. **What should you do if you encounter a flooded roadway while driving in Ohio?**

A. ▢ Drive through the water as quickly as possible

B. ▢ Stop and wait for the water to recede

C. ▢ Find an alternate route to avoid the flooded area

D. ▢ Continue driving through the water at a slow and steady pace

8. **What should you do if your vehicle catches fire while driving in Ohio?**

A. ▢ Exit the vehicle immediately and move a safe distance away

B. ▢ Continue driving to the nearest gas station to get help

C. ▢ Open the hood and pour water on the engine to put out the fire

D. ▢ Call 911 and wait in the vehicle for help to arrive

9. **What should you do if you encounter a deer or other large animal on the roadway in Ohio?**

A. ▢ Swerve to avoid the animal

B. ▢ Hit the animal head-on to minimize damage to your vehicle

C. ▢ Brake hard and come to a stop

D. ▢ Honk your horn and continue driving at the same speed

10. What should you do if you are caught in a snowstorm while driving in Ohio?

A. ▢ Turn off your headlights to avoid glare

B. ▢ Increase your speed to get through the storm more quickly

C. ▢ Pull over to a safe location and wait for the storm to pass

D. ▢ Continue driving as normal

11. Turn your steering wheel sharply to avoid the skid

A. ▢ Keep driving and ignore the accident

B. ▢ Call 911 to report the accident and continue driving

C. ▢ Stop and offer reasonable assistance, such as calling for medical help

D. ▢ Stop and offer to tow the vehicles involved to a nearby garage

12. What should you do if your vehicle begins to hydroplane while driving in Ohio?

A. ▢ Brake hard to try to regain control

B. ▢ Turn off your engine to slow down

C. ▢ Steer in the direction of the skid

D. ▢ Turn your steering wheel sharply to avoid the skid

13. What should you do if you are experiencing a medical emergency while driving in Ohio?

A. ▢ Continue driving to the nearest hospital

B. ▢ Pull over to a safe location and call for medical help

C. ▢ Ask a passenger to take over driving

D. ▢ Ignore the situation and continue driving as normal

14. What should you do if your accelerator becomes stuck while driving in Ohio?

A. ▢ Slam on the brakes to try to stop the vehicle

B. ▢ Turn off the engine to stop the vehicle

C. ▢ Shift into neutral and use the brakes to bring the vehicle to a stop

D. ▢ Continue driving at a high speed until you reach a safe location

15. What should you do if you come across a traffic signal that is not working in Ohio?

A. ▢ Drive through the intersection as quickly as possible

B. ▢ Treat the intersection as a four-way stop

C. ▢ Ignore the intersection and continue driving

D. ▢ Honk your horn to alert other drivers

Correct answers for emergencies exam

1. C. Stop your vehicle and remain at the scene until law enforcement arrives

2. C. Stop and pull over to the right side of the road.

3. C. Pull over to a safe location and wait for the storm to pass

4. A. Slow down and brake gently

5. B. Pull over to a safe location and call for medical help

6. D. Turn off the engine to slow down

7. C. Find an alternate route to avoid the flooded area

8. A. Exit the vehicle immediately and move a safe distance away

9. C. Brake hard and come to a stop

10. C. Pull over to a safe location and wait for the storm to pass

11. C. Stop and offer reasonable assistance, such as calling for medical help

12. C. Steer in the direction of the skid

13. B. Pull over to a safe location and call for medical help

14. C. Shift into neutral and use the brakes to bring the vehicle to a stop

15. B. Treat the intersection as a four-way stop

Emergencies exam 2

1. **What should you do if you come across a downed power line in Ohio?**

    A. ▫ Touch it to see if it's live

    B. ▫ Move it out of the way

    C. ▫ Call your utility company or emergency services to report it and stay at least 30 feet away

    D. ▫ Ignore it and continue on your way

2. **What should you do if you see a tornado warning in Ohio?**

    A. ▫ Go outside and watch the storm

    B. ▫ Stay indoors and stay away from windows

    C. ▫ Drive to a nearby shelter

    D. ▫ Call your friends to tell them about the storm

3. **What should you do if you encounter a flash flood in Ohio?**

    A. ▫ Drive through it quickly to get to your destination

    B. ▫ Abandon your car and seek higher ground

    C. ▫ Take shelter in your car until the water recedes

    D. ▫ Stand outside to watch the floodwaters

4. **What should you do if you come into contact with a poisonous plant in Ohio?**

    A. ▫ Ignore it and continue on your way

    B. ▫ Wash the affected area with soap and water

    C. ▫ Apply a topical cream to the area

    D. ▫ Wait for the symptoms to go away on their own

5. **What should you do if you witness a car accident in Ohio?**

A. ▫ Call 911 and try to provide first aid to anyone who is injured

B. ▫ Drive around the accident and continue on your way

C. ▫ Honk your horn to get people's attention

D. ▫ Take pictures of the accident for your social media accounts

6. **What should you do if you smell gas inside your home in Ohio?**

A. ▫ Light a match to find the source of the smell

B. ▫ Open windows and doors to ventilate the area

C. ▫ Turn on all of your home's lights

D. ▫ Turn off your gas supply and call your gas company

7. **What should you do if you hear a fire alarm in Ohio?**

A. ▫ Ignore it and continue on your way

B. ▫ Investigate the source of the alarm

C. ▫ Evacuate the building immediately

D. ▫ Call your friends to tell them about the alarm

8. **What should you do if you encounter a bear in Ohio?**

A. ▫ Run away as fast as you can

B. ▫ Yell at the bear to scare it off

C. ▫ Play dead and wait for the bear to leave

D. ▫ Slowly back away and avoid eye contact

9. **What should you do if you see someone experiencing a heat stroke in Ohio?**

A. ▢ Give them a hot drink to rehydrate them

B. ▢ Apply cold compresses to their forehead and neck

C. ▢ Take them to a sauna to cool down

D. ▢ Ignore them and continue on your way

10. What should you do if you witness a crime in Ohio?

A. ▢ Call 911 and report the crime

B. ▢ Ignore it and continue on your way

C. ▢ Confront the perpetrator yourself

D. ▢ Take pictures or videos to share on social media

11. What should you do if you encounter a power outage in Ohio?

A. ▢ Light candles and start a fire for warmth

B. ▢ Call your utility company to report the outage and stay away from fallen power lines

C. ▢ Attempt to fix the issue yourself by checking your circuit breaker

D. ▢ Use a generator to restore power to your home

12. What should you do if you encounter a blizzard in Ohio?

A. ▢ Venture outside to take pictures of the snow

B. ▢ Stay indoors and limit travel to emergencies only

C. ▢ Drive to a nearby shelter for warmth

D. ▢ Go out and enjoy the winter weather

13. What should you do if you encounter a medical emergency in Ohio?

A. ▢ Ignore the situation and hope it resolves itself

B. ▢ Call 911 or seek medical attention immediately

C. ▢ Wait and see if the person improves on their own

D. ▢ Administer your own medical care to the person in need

14. What should you do if you smell smoke inside your home in Ohio?

A. ▢ Investigate the source of the smell

B. ▢ Light a candle to mask the smell

C. ▢ Turn off your smoke detectors to avoid false alarms

D. ▢ Open windows and doors to ventilate the area

15. What should you do if you encounter a hazardous material spill in Ohio?

A. ▢ Take pictures or videos to share on social media

B. ▢ Ignore the spill and continue on your way

C. ▢ Call 911 and report the spill

D. ▢ Attempt to clean up the spill yourself

Correct answers for emergencies exam 2

1. **C.** Call your utility company or emergency services to report it and stay at least 30 feet away

2. **B.** Stay indoors and stay away from windows

3. **B.** Abandon your car and seek higher ground

4. **B.** Wash the affected area with soap and water

5. **A.** Call 911 and try to provide first aid to anyone who is injured

6. **D.** Turn off your gas supply and call your gas company

7. **C.** Evacuate the building immediately

8. **D.** Slowly back away and avoid eye contact

9. **B.** Apply cold compresses to their forehead and neck

10. **A.** Call 911 and report the crime

11. **B.** Call your utility company to report the outage and stay away from fallen power lines

12. **B.** Stay indoors and limit travel to emergencies only

13. **B.** Call 911 or seek medical attention immediately

14. **A.** Investigate the source of the smell

15. **C.** Call 911 and report the spill

Emergencies exam 3

1. **What should you do if you encounter a tornado in Ohio?**

    A. ▢ Stay inside and take shelter in an interior room on the lowest level of your building

    B. ▢ Venture outside to take pictures or videos of the tornado

    C. ▢ Drive towards the tornado to get a closer look

    D. ▢ Seek shelter in your car

2. **What should you do if you encounter a flash flood in Ohio?**

    A. ▢ Attempt to drive through the flood waters to reach your destination

    B. ▢ Stay indoors and wait for the water to recede

    C. ▢ Evacuate to higher ground if advised to do so by authorities

    D. ▢ Wade through the flood waters to get to safety

3. **What should you do if you encounter a gas leak in Ohio?**

    A. ▢ Attempt to fix the leak yourself

    B. ▢ Light a match to try and find the source of the leak

    C. ▢ Open windows and doors to ventilate the area

    D. ▢ Evacuate the building and call 911

4. **What should you do if you encounter a wildfire in Ohio?**

    A. ▢ Take pictures or videos of the fire for social media

    B. ▢ Attempt to put the fire out yourself

    C. ▢ Evacuate the area if advised to do so by authorities

    D. ▢ Start a controlled burn to prevent the fire from spreading

5. **What should you do if you encounter a power line down in Ohio?**

   A. ▢ Touch the power line to see if it's live

   B. ▢ Drive over the power line to get to your destination

   C. ▢ Call 911 and stay away from the power line

   D. ▢ Attempt to move the power line out of the way

6. **What should you do if you encounter a house fire in Ohio?**

   A. ▢ Call 911 and evacuate the building

   B. ▢ Attempt to put out the fire yourself

   C. ▢ Move all your valuables to a safe location

   D. ▢ Stay in your room and close the door to prevent smoke from entering

7. **What should you do if you encounter a heat wave in Ohio?**

   A. ▢ Stay indoors and limit outdoor activity during the hottest parts of the day

   B. ▢ Spend as much time outside as possible to enjoy the weather

   C. ▢ Wear dark, heavy clothing to absorb the sun's rays

   D. ▢ Turn off your air conditioning to save energy

8. **What should you do if you encounter a terrorist attack in Ohio?**

   A. ▢ Ignore the situation and continue with your day

   B. ▢ Call 911 and report any suspicious activity or packages

   C. ▢ Confront the attackers and try to reason with them

   D. ▢ Run towards the scene to take pictures or videos

9. **What should you do if you encounter a severe thunderstorm in Ohio?**

   A. ▢ Stay indoors and avoid using electrical appliances

198

B. ▫ Go outside and watch the storm

C. ▫ Attempt to drive through flooded streets

D. ▫ Run in an open area to avoid getting hit by lightning

10. What should you do if you encounter a snowstorm in Ohio?

A. ▫ Venture outside to enjoy the winter weather

B. ▫ Stay indoors and limit travel to emergencies only

C. ▫ Attempt to drive in the snow without snow tires or chains

D. ▫ Open windows and doors to ventilate the area

11. What should you do if you encounter a vehicle accident in Ohio?

A. ▫ Take pictures or videos of the accident for social media

B. ▫ Attempt to move the injured persons

C. ▫ Call 911 and provide details about the accident and any injuries

D. ▫ Ignore the accident and continue on your way

12. What should you do if you encounter a power outage in Ohio?

A. ▫ Light candles to brighten your home

B. ▫ Use a generator inside your home to power your appliances

C. ▫ Unplug your appliances to prevent damage from a power surge

D. ▫ Contact your utility company to report the outage

13. What should you do if you encounter a severe winter storm in Ohio?

A. ▫ Go outside and enjoy the winter weather

B. ▫ Stay indoors and limit travel to emergencies only

C. ▫ Attempt to drive without snow tires or chains

D. ▢ Keep your windows and doors open to ventilate the area

14. What should you do if you encounter a building collapse in Ohio?

    A. ▢ Enter the building to search for anyone who may be trapped

    B. ▢ Call 911 and report the incident

    C. ▢ Attempt to rescue anyone trapped yourself

    D. ▢ Ignore the incident and continue on your way

15. What should you do if you encounter a hazardous material exposure in Ohio?

    A. ▢ Ignore the exposure and continue with your day

    B. ▢ Call 911 and report the exposure

    C. ▢ Attempt to treat the exposure yourself

    D. ▢ Move to a different area to avoid the exposure

Correct answers for emergencies exam 3

1. **A.** Stay inside and take shelter in an interior room on the lowest level of your building
2. **C.** Evacuate to higher ground if advised to do so by authorities
3. **D.** Evacuate the building and call 911
4. **C.** Evacuate the area if advised to do so by authorities
5. **C.** Call 911 and stay away from the power line
6. **A.** Call 911 and evacuate the building
7. **A.** Stay indoors and limit outdoor activity during the hottest parts of the day
8. **B.** Call 911 and report any suspicious activity or packages
9. **A.** Stay indoors and avoid using electrical appliance
10. **B.** Stay indoors and limit travel to emergencies only
11. **C.** Call 911 and provide details about the accident and any injuries
12. **D.** Contact your utility company to report the outage
13. **B.** Stay indoors and limit travel to emergencies only
14. **B.** Call 911 and report the incident
15. **B.** Call 911 and report the exposure

Emergencies exam 4

1. **What should you do if you encounter a hazardous material spill in Ohio?**

    A. ▢ Approach the spill to investigate the type of material

    B. ▢ Ignore the spill and continue on your way

    C. ▢ Call 911 and report the spill, then evacuate the area if necessary

    D. ▢ Attempt to clean up the spill yourself

2. **What should you do if you encounter a severe thunderstorm warning in Ohio?**

    A. ▢ Stay outside to watch the storm

    B. ▢ Go to a nearby park to watch the storm

    C. ▢ Move to a sturdy building or vehicle, and avoid windows

    D. ▢ Drive to a nearby hilltop to observe the storm

3. **What should you do if you encounter a large-scale disaster, such as a terrorist attack, in Ohio?**

    A. ▢ Go to the location of the disaster to help

    B. ▢ Ignore the disaster and continue on your way

    C. ▢ Call 911 and follow the instructions provided

    D. ▢ Post about the disaster on social media

4. **What should you do if you encounter a carbon monoxide leak in Ohio?**

    A. ▢ Ignore the leak and continue on your way

    B. ▢ Ventilate the area by opening windows and doors

    C. ▢ Attempt to fix the leak yourself

    D. ▢ Evacuate the area and call 911

5. **What should you do if you encounter a winter storm warning in Ohio?**

   A. ▢ Drive faster to get to your destination before the storm arrives

   B. ▢ Stay at home and avoid travel if possible

   C. ▢ Go outside to observe the snowfall

   D. ▢ Drive slowly and without urgency during the storm

6. **What should you do if you encounter a power outage in Ohio?**

   A. ▢ Attempt to fix the issue yourself

   B. ▢ Call 911 to report the outage

   C. ▢ Use candles for light instead of flashlights

   D. ▢ Turn on all appliances to see if power is restored

7. **What should you do if you suspect someone is experiencing a heart attack in Ohio?**

   A. ▢ Give them aspirin to chew

   B. ▢ Encourage them to lie down and rest

   C. ▢ Call 911 immediately

   D. ▢ Administer CPR

8. **What should you do if you encounter a downed power line in Ohio?**

   A. ▢ Touch the power line to see if it is still live

   B. ▢ Move the power line out of the way so that you can continue on your way

   C. ▢ Call the power company to report the downed power line

   D. ▢ Attempt to repair the power line yourself

9. **During a flood in Ohio, what should you do if you are told to evacuate?**

   A. ▢ Refuse to leave your home and wait for the flood to pass

B. ▢ Move to the highest floor of your home

C. ▢ Follow evacuation orders and move to higher ground or a shelter

D. ▢ Try to build a barrier around your home to prevent water from entering

10. **In Ohio, which of the following natural disasters is most likely to cause a state of emergency to be declared?**

    A. ▢ Heavy snowfall

    B. ▢ Thunderstorms

    C. ▢ Tornadoes

    D. ▢ Wildfires

11. **In Ohio, what is the main reason for a public health emergency to be declared?**

    A. ▢ A new strain of the flu has been discovered.

    B. ▢ A large-scale foodborne illness outbreak has occurred.

    C. ▢ A terrorist attack has taken place in the state.

    D. ▢ A local hospital has experienced a power outage.

12. **In Ohio, which of the following events could result in a mandatory evacuation order?**

    A. ▢ A chemical spill in a remote area

    B. ▢ A small-scale house fire

    C. ▢ A power outage affecting a neighborhood

    D. ▢ A massive flood in a populated area

13. **In Ohio, which of the following disasters is most likely to cause a Level 3 emergency response?**

    A. ▢ A car accident involving hazardous materials

    B. ▢ A severe thunderstorm

    C. ▢ A house fire

D. ▢ A water main break

14. In Ohio, what is the primary purpose of a Level 2 emergency response?

A. ▢ To ensure public safety and property protection

B. ▢ To provide immediate medical assistance to injured individuals

C. ▢ To evacuate affected residents from the disaster area

D. ▢ To contain the spread of a contagious disease outbreak

15. In Ohio, which of the following is an example of a Level 1 emergency response?

A. ▢ A gas leak in a commercial building

B. ▢ A power outage affecting a small number of homes

C. ▢ A minor car accident with no injuries

D. ▢ A small kitchen fire in a restaurant

Correct answers for emergencies exam 4

1. **C.** Call 911 and report the spill, then evacuate the area if necessary

2. **C.** Move to a sturdy building or vehicle, and avoid windows

3. **C.** Call 911 and follow the instructions provided

4. **D.** Evacuate the area and call 911

5. **B.** Stay at home and avoid travel if possible

6. **B.** Call 911 to report the outage

7. **C.** Call 911 immediately

8. **C.** Call the power company to report the downed power line

9. **C.** Follow evacuation orders and move to higher ground or a shelter

10. **C.** Tornadoes

11. **B.** A large-scale foodborne illness outbreak has occurred.

12. **D.** A massive flood in a populated area

13. **A.** A car accident involving hazardous materials

14. **A.** To ensure public safety and property protection

15. **D.** A small kitchen fire in a restaurant

Emergencies exam 5

1. **In Ohio, what is the primary purpose of the Emergency Alert System (EAS)?**

   A. ▢ To provide information and instructions to the public during an emergency

   B. ▢ To coordinate emergency response efforts between local agencies

   C. ▢ To transport injured individuals to hospitals and medical facilities

   D. ▢ To provide shelter and food to affected residents

2. **During a Level 2 emergency response in Ohio, what is the primary responsibility of local government officials?**

   A. ▢ To provide immediate medical assistance to injured individuals

   B. ▢ To evacuate affected residents from the disaster area

   C. ▢ To provide shelter and food to displaced individuals

   D. ▢ To coordinate emergency response efforts with state and federal agencies

3. **In Ohio, what agency is responsible for managing and coordinating disaster recovery efforts?**

   A. ▢ Federal Emergency Management Agency (FEMA)

   B. ▢ Ohio Emergency Management Agency (OEMA)

   C. ▢ Ohio Department of Transportation (ODOT)

   D. ▢ Ohio Environmental Protection Agency (OEPA)

4. **Which of the following is an example of a Level 1 emergency response in Ohio?**

   A. ▢ A house fire in a residential neighborhood

   B. ▢ A gas leak in a commercial building

   C. ▢ A small-scale power outage affecting a few homes

   D. ▢ A minor car accident with no injuries

5. **During a Level 3 emergency response in Ohio, what agency has the primary responsibility for providing emergency medical services?**

A. ▢ Ohio Department of Transportation (ODOT)

B. ▢ Ohio Environmental Protection Agency (OEPA)

C. ▢ Ohio State Highway Patrol (OSHP)

D. ▢ Local emergency medical services (EMS) agencies

6. **In Ohio, what agency is responsible for managing and coordinating the state's response to acts of terrorism?**

A. ▢ Ohio Emergency Management Agency (OEMA)

B. ▢ Ohio Department of Public Safety (ODPS)

C. ▢ Ohio Homeland Security (OHS)

D. ▢ Ohio State Highway Patrol (OSHP)

7. **In Ohio, what agency is responsible for coordinating disaster response efforts with non-governmental organizations (NGOs)?**

A. ▢ To provide search and rescue operations

B. ▢ To assist with medical evacuation efforts

C. ▢ To provide law enforcement and security support

D. ▢ To distribute emergency supplies and resources

8. **In Ohio, what agency is responsible for coordinating disaster response efforts with non-governmental organizations (NGOs)?**

A. ▢ Ohio Emergency Management Agency (OEMA)

B. ▢ Ohio Department of Transportation (ODOT)

C. ▢ Ohio Environmental Protection Agency (OEPA)

D. ▢ Ohio Voluntary Organizations Active in Disaster (VOAD)

9. **During a Level 3 emergency response in Ohio, what is the recommended course of action for individuals with mobility issues?**

A. ▢ Stay indoors and monitor local media for updates

B. ▢ Evacuate the area immediately and follow official instructions

C. ▢ Call 911 and request assistance from emergency responders

D. ▢ Seek shelter in a designated safe location

10. **Which of the following is an example of a Level 3 emergency response in Ohio?**

A. ▢ A small-scale power outage affecting a few homes

B. ▢ A house fire in a residential neighborhood

C. ▢ A hazardous materials spill on a major highway

D. ▢ A severe thunderstorm with high winds and heavy rain

11. **What is the primary purpose of the Ohio Emergency Operations Center (EOC)?**

A. ▢ To provide shelter for affected residents

B. ▢ To provide shelter for affected residents

C. ▢ To distribute emergency supplies and resources

D. ▢ To conduct damage assessments after a disaster

12. **During a Level 3 emergency response in Ohio, what is the recommended course of action for the public?**

A. ▢ Shelter in place and turn off all ventilation systems

B. ▢ Evacuate the area immediately and follow official instructions

C. ▢ Call 911 and report any hazards or dangerous conditions

D. ▢ Stay indoors and monitor local media for updates

13. In Ohio, what agency is responsible for responding to hazardous materials incidents?

A. ▢ Ohio Emergency Management Agency (OEMA)

B. ▢ Ohio Department of Transportation (ODOT)

C. ▢ Ohio Environmental Protection Agency (OEPA)

D. ▢ Ohio State Highway Patrol (OSHP)

14. Which of the following natural disasters is least likely to occur in Ohio?

A. ▢ Tornado

B. ▢ Flood

C. ▢ Hurricane

D. ▢ Earthquake

15. In Ohio, which agency is responsible for issuing severe weather alerts and warnings?

A. ▢ National Weather Service (NWS)

B. ▢ Ohio Department of Natural Resources (ODNR)

C. ▢ Ohio Environmental Protection Agency (OEPA)

D. ▢ Ohio Department of Transportation (ODOT)

Correct answers for emergencies exam 5

1. **A.** To provide information and instructions to the public during an emergency
2. **D.** To coordinate emergency response efforts with state and federal agencies
3. **B.** Ohio Emergency Management Agency (OEMA)
4. **D.** A minor car accident with no injuries
5. **D.** Local emergency medical services (EMS) agencies
6. **C.** Ohio Homeland Security (OHS)
7. **C.** To provide law enforcement and security support
8. **D.** Ohio Voluntary Organizations Active in Disaster (VOAD)
9. **C.** Call 911 and request assistance from emergency responders
10. **C.** A hazardous materials spill on a major highway
11. **A.** To coordinate emergency response efforts
12. **B.** Evacuate the area immediately and follow official instructions
13. **A.** Ohio Emergency Management Agency (OEMA)
14. **C.** Hurricane
15. **A.** National Weather Service (NWS)

Vehicle size and weight limits

The Ohio Department of Motor Vehicles (DMV) sets specific size and weight limits for vehicles operating on Ohio's roadways. These limits are in place to ensure the safety of all motorists on the road, as well as to protect the integrity of the state's roadways and bridges.

Understanding the size and weight limits is essential for all drivers, particularly those operating commercial vehicles, as they are subject to more stringent regulations than passenger vehicles. Failure to adhere to these regulations can result in costly fines, vehicle impoundment, and even legal action in the event of an accident.

This chapter will provide an overview of Ohio's vehicle size and weight limits, including the maximum limits for various vehicle types, the permitted weight for different axles, and the procedures for obtaining permits to operate overweight or oversized vehicles. Additionally, this chapter will cover the penalties associated with violating these limits and provide tips for staying safe and compliant on Ohio's roadways.

By the end of this chapter, you should have a comprehensive understanding of Ohio's vehicle size and weight limits and be equipped with the knowledge needed to ensure safe and legal operation of vehicles on Ohio's roads.

For training purposes, you can mark the ▢ symbol next to what you think is the correct answer: Once you have chosen the correct answer, use a pencil or pen to mark the ▢ symbol next to that answer.

So, let's get started!

Vehicle size and weight limits exam

1. **What is the maximum legal width for a vehicle operating on Ohio's roadways?**

   A. ▢ 7 feet

   B. ▢ 8 feet

   C. ▢ 9 feet

   D. ▢ 10 feet

2. **What is the maximum legal weight for a single axle on a commercial vehicle in Ohio?**

   A. ▢ 12,000 pounds

   B. ▢ 18,000 pounds

   C. ▢ 20,000 pounds

   D. ▢ 25,000 pounds

3. **What is the maximum legal height for a vehicle, including load and accessories, operating on Ohio's roadways?**

   A. ▢ 12 feet

   B. ▢ 13 feet 6 inches

   C. ▢ 14 feet

   D. ▢ 15 feet

4. **What is the maximum legal length for a single vehicle operating on Ohio's roadways?**

   A. ▢ 45 feet

   B. ▢ 50 feet

   C. ▢ 60 feet

   D. ▢ 70 feet

5. **When must a driver obtain a special permit to operate an overweight or oversized vehicle on Ohio's roadways?**

A. ▢ When the vehicle weighs more than 80,000 pounds

B. ▢ When the vehicle exceeds the legal length or width limits

C. ▢ When the vehicle is carrying hazardous materials

D. ▢ All of the above

6. **What is the maximum legal weight for a tandem axle on a commercial vehicle in Ohio?**

A. ▢ 34,000 pounds

B. ▢ 36,000 pounds

C. ▢ 38,000 pounds

D. ▢ 40,000 pounds

7. **What is the maximum legal weight for a commercial vehicle on Ohio's interstate highways?**

A. ▢ 80,000 pounds

B. ▢ 82,000 pounds

C. ▢ 85,000 pounds

D. ▢ 90,000 pounds

8. **What is the maximum legal length for a combination of vehicles operating on Ohio's roadways?**

A. ▢ 65 feet

B. ▢ 75 feet

C. ▢ 80 feet

D. ▢ 90 feet

9. **What is the maximum legal weight for a commercial vehicle on Ohio's non-interstate highways?**

A. ▢ 73,280 pounds

B. ▢ 73,000 pounds

C. ▢ 72,000 pounds

D. ▢ 71,280 pounds

10. What is the maximum legal weight for a commercial vehicle with three or more axles on Ohio's roadways?

A. ▢ 48,000 pounds

B. ▢ 54,000 pounds

C. ▢ 60,000 pounds

D. ▢ 66,000 pounds

11. What is the maximum allowed weight for a single axle on Ohio's interstate highways?

A. ▢ 20,000 pounds

B. ▢ 22,000 pounds

C. ▢ 24,000 pounds

D. ▢ 26,000 pounds

12. What is the maximum allowed weight for a vehicle on Ohio's non-interstate highways?

A. ▢ 80,000 pounds

B. ▢ 86,000 pounds

C. ▢ 90,000 pounds

D. ▢ 96,000 pounds

13. What is the maximum allowable weight for a combination of a truck and trailer with 4 axles in Ohio?

A. ▢ 60,000 pounds

B. ▢ 65,000 pounds

C. ▢ 70,000 pounds

D. ▢ 75,000 pounds

14. What is the maximum width allowed for a vehicle on Ohio's highways?

A. ▢ 8 feet 6 inches

B. ▢ 9 feet

C. ▢ 10 feet

D. ▢ 11 feet

15. What is the maximum weight allowed for a single axle on Ohio's county roads?

A. ▢ 16,000 pounds

B. ▢ 18,000 pounds

C. ▢ 20,000 pounds

D. ▢ 22,000 pounds

Correct answers for vehicle size and weight limits exam

1. **B.** 8 feet
2. **B.** 18,000 pounds
3. **B.** 13 feet 6 inches
4. **B.** 50 feet
5. **D.** All of the above
6. **C.** 38,000 pounds
7. **B.** 82,000 pounds
8. **C.** 80 feet
9. **A.** 73,280 pounds
10. **B.** 54,000 pounds
11. **C.** 24,000 pounds
12. **B.** 86,000 pounds
13. **C.** 70,000 pounds
14. **A.** 8 feet 6 inches
15. **A.** 16,000 pounds

Vehicle size and weight limits exam 2

1. **What is the maximum weight allowed for a single axle on Ohio's county roads?**

   A. ▢ 16,000 pounds

   B. ▢ 18,000 pounds

   C. ▢ 20,000 pounds

   D. ▢ 22,000 pounds

2. **What is the maximum height allowed for a vehicle on Ohio's national network of highways?**

   A. ▢ 12 feet

   B. ▢ 13 feet

   C. ▢ 14 feet

   D. ▢ 15 feet

3. **What is the maximum length allowed for a combination of vehicles on Ohio's national network of highways?**

   A. ▢ 75 feet

   B. ▢ 80 feet

   C. ▢ 85 feet

   D. ▢ 90 feet

4. **What is the maximum allowed weight for a vehicle on Ohio's urban interstate highways?**

   A. ▢ 73,280 pounds

   B. ▢ 80,000 pounds

   C. ▢ 86,000 pounds

   D. ▢ 88,000 pounds

5. **What is the maximum length allowed for a vehicle combination of two trailers on Ohio's highways?**

A. ◻ 65 feet

B. ◻ 70 feet

C. ◻ 75 feet

D. ◻ 80 feet

6. **What is the maximum weight allowed for a single axle on Ohio's non-interstate highways?**

A. ◻ 16,000 pounds

B. ◻ 18,000 pounds

C. ◻ 20,000 pounds

D. ◻ 22,000 pounds

7. **What is the maximum combined weight allowed for a truck and trailer on Ohio's highways?**

A. ◻ 70,000 pounds

B. ◻ 80,000 pounds

C. ◻ 90,000 pounds

D. ◻ 100,000 pounds

8. **What is the maximum length allowed for a single vehicle on Ohio's highways?**

A. ◻ 40 feet

B. ◻ 45 feet

C. ◻ 50 feet

D. ◻ 55 feet

9. **What is the maximum length allowed for a trailer on Ohio's highways?**

219

A. □ 48 feet

B. □ 53 feet

C. □ 58 feet

D. □ 63 feet

10. What is the maximum weight limit for a tandem axle vehicle in most states?

A. □ 34,000 pounds

B. □ 36,000 pounds

C. □ 38,000 pounds

D. □ 40,000 pounds

11. What is the maximum height limit for a vehicle in the United States?

A. □ 12 feet

B. □ 13 feet

C. □ 14 feet

D. □ 15 feet

12. What is the maximum allowable weight for a two-axle vehicle in Ohio?

A. □ 34,000 pounds

B. □ 36,000 pounds

C. □ 38,000 pounds

D. □ 40,000 pounds

13. What is the maximum allowable weight for a combination of a truck and trailer with 5 axles in Ohio without a permit?

A. □ 90,000 pounds

B. ▢ 92,000 pounds

C. ▢ 94,000 pounds

D. ▢ 96,000 pounds

14. What is the maximum allowable width for a vehicle in Ohio?

A. ▢ 8 feet

B. ▢ 8.5 feet

C. ▢ 9 feet

D. ▢ 9.5 feet

15. What is the maximum allowable weight for a combination of a truck and trailer with 5 or more axles in Ohio?

A. ▢ 80,000 pounds

B. ▢ 85,000 pounds

C. ▢ 90,000 pounds

D. ▢ 95,000 pounds

Correct answers for vehicle size and weight limits exam 2

1. **A**. 16,000 pounds
2. **C**. 14 feet
3. **D**. 90 feet
4. **D**. 88,000 pounds
5. **A**. 65 feet
6. **B**. 18,000 pounds
7. **B**. 80,000 pounds
8. **D**. 55 feet
9. **B**. 53 feet
10. **B**. 36,000 pounds
11. **B**. 13 feet
12. **B**. 36,000 pounds
13. **A**. 90,000 pounds
14. **B**. 8.5 feet
15. **C**. 90,000 pounds

Vehicle size and weight limits exam 3

1. **What is the maximum allowable weight for a three-axle vehicle in Ohio?**

   A. ▢ 48,000 pounds

   B. ▢ 50,000 pounds

   C. ▢ 52,000 pounds

   D. ▢ 54,000 pounds

2. **What is the maximum allowable length for a combination of a truck and trailer in Ohio?**

   A. ▢ 80,000 pounds

   B. ▢ 82,000 pounds

   C. ▢ 84,000 pounds

   D. ▢ 86,000 pounds

3. **What is the maximum allowable length for a combination of a truck and trailer in Ohio?**

   A. ▢ 65 feet

   B. ▢ 70 feet

   C. ▢ 75 feet

   D. ▢ 80 feet

4. **What is the maximum allowable weight for a combination of a truck and trailer with 6 axles in Ohio?**

   A. ▢ 110,000 pounds

   B. ▢ 120,000 pounds

   C. ▢ 130,000 pounds

   D. ▢ 140,000 pounds

5. **What is the maximum allowable width for a vehicle in Ohio with a permit?**

A. ▢ 10 feet

B. ▢ 11 feet

C. ▢ 12 feet

D. ▢ 13 feet

6. **What is the maximum allowable weight for a four-axle vehicle in Ohio on interstate highways?**

A. ▢ 68,000 pounds

B. ▢ 70,000 pounds

C. ▢ 72,000 pounds

D. ▢ 74,000 pounds

7. **What is the maximum allowable height for a vehicle in Ohio with a permit?**

A. ▢ 14 feet

B. ▢ 15 feet

C. ▢ 16 feet

D. ▢ 17 feet

8. **What is the maximum allowable weight for a combination of a truck and trailer with 7 axles in Ohio?**

A. ▢ 138,000 pounds

B. ▢ 148,000 pounds

C. ▢ 158,000 pounds

D. ▢ 168,000 pounds

9. What is the maximum allowable weight for a three-axle vehicle on non-interstate highways in Ohio?

A. ▫ 45,000 pounds

B. ▫ 47,000 pounds

C. ▫ 49,000 pounds

D. ▫ 51,000 pounds

10. What is the maximum allowable weight for a six-axle vehicle on non-interstate highways in Ohio?

A. ▫ 86,000 pounds

B. ▫ 88,000 pounds

C. ▫ 90,000 pounds

D. ▫ 92,000 pounds

11. What is the maximum allowable length for a combination of a truck and trailer with 4 axles in Ohio without a permit?

A. ▫ 70 feet

B. ▫ 75 feet

C. ▫ 80 feet

D. ▫ 85 feet

12. What is the maximum allowable weight for a single axle vehicle on interstate highways in Ohio?

A. ▫ 18,000 pounds

B. ▫ 20,000 pounds

C. ▫ 22,000 pounds

D. ▫ 24,000 pounds

13. **What is the maximum allowable weight for a single axle vehicle on non-interstate highways in Ohio?**

A. ▢ 18,000 pounds

B. ▢ 20,000 pounds

C. ▢ 22,000 pounds

D. ▢ 24,000 pounds

14. **What is the maximum allowable weight for a combination of a truck and trailer with 6 axles in Ohio on interstate highways?**

A. ▢ 98,000 pounds

B. ▢ 100,000 pounds

C. ▢ 102,000 pounds

D. ▢ 104,000 pounds

15. **What is the maximum allowable weight for a three-axle vehicle on interstate highways in Ohio?**

A. ▢ 54,000 pounds

B. ▢ 56,000 pounds

C. ▢ 58,000 pounds

D. ▢ 60,000 pounds

Correct answers for vehicle size and weight limits exam 3

1. **A.** 48,000 pounds
2. **B.** 82,000 pounds
3. **B.** 70 feet
4. **B.** 120,000 pounds
5. **B.** 20,000 pounds
6. **C.** 72,000 pounds
7. **C.** 16 feet
8. **A.** 138,000 pounds
9. **D.** 51,000 pounds
10. **A.** 86,000 pounds
11. **B.** 75 feet
12. **B.** 20,000 pounds
13. **C.** 22,000 pounds
14. **B.** 100,000 pounds
15. **D.** 60,000 pounds

Vehicle size and weight limits exam 4

1. What is the maximum allowable length for a combination of a truck and trailer with 5 axles in Ohio with a permit?

   A. ▢ 95 feet

   B. ▢ 100 feet

   C. ▢ 105 feet

   D. ▢ 110 feet

2. What is the maximum allowable length for a single vehicle on Ohio highways without a permit?

   A. ▢ 40 feet

   B. ▢ 45 feet

   C. ▢ 50 feet

   D. ▢ 55 feet

3. What is the maximum allowable weight for a five-axle vehicle on interstate highways in Ohio?

   A. ▢ 72,000 pounds

   B. ▢ 74,000 pounds

   C. ▢ 76,000 pounds

   D. ▢ 78,000 pounds

4. What is the maximum allowable weight for a combination of a truck and trailer with 7 axles in Ohio on non-interstate highways?

   A. ▢ 102,000 pounds

   B. ▢ 104,000 pounds

   C. ▢ 106,000 pounds

D. ▫ 108,000 pounds

5. What is the maximum allowable height for a vehicle in Ohio with a permit?

A. ▫ 13 feet

B. ▫ 14 feet

C. ▫ 15 feet

D. ▫ 16 feet

6. What is the maximum allowable weight for a single-axle vehicle on Ohio highways without a permit?

A. ▫ 12,000 pounds

B. ▫ 15,000 pounds

C. ▫ 18,000 pounds

D. ▫ 20,000 pounds

7. What is the maximum allowable length for a single vehicle on non-interstate highways in Ohio without a permit?

A. ▫ 40 feet

B. ▫ 45 feet

C. ▫ 50 feet

D. ▫ 55 feet

8. What is the maximum weight limit for a vehicle with five axles traveling on US interstates?

A. ▫ 80,000 pounds

B. ▫ 84,000 pounds

C. ▫ 88,000 pounds

D. ▫ 92,000 pounds

9. What is the maximum weight limit for a vehicle with five axles traveling on US highways?

A. ▢ 76,000 pounds

B. ▢ 80,000 pounds

C. ▢ 84,000 pounds

D. ▢ 88,000 pounds

10. What is the maximum allowable weight for a combination of a truck and trailer with 4 axles in Ohio without a permit?

A. ▢ 62,000 pounds

B. ▢ 64,000 pounds

C. ▢ 66,000 pounds

D. ▢ 68,000 pounds

11. What is the maximum allowable weight for a three-axle vehicle on Ohio Turnpike?

A. ▢ 48,000 pounds

B. ▢ 50,000 pounds

C. ▢ 52,000 pounds

D. ▢ 54,000 pounds

12. What is the maximum allowable weight for a combination of a truck and trailer with 2 axles in Ohio on interstate highways?

A. ▢ 36,000 pounds

B. ▢ 38,000 pounds

C. ▢ 40,000 pounds

D. ▢ 42,000 pounds

13. What is the maximum allowable weight for a combination of a truck and trailer with 3 axles in Ohio without a permit?

A. ▢ 48,000 pounds

B. ▢ 50,000 pounds

C. ▢ 52,000 pounds

D. ▢ 54,000 pounds

14. What is the maximum allowable weight for a combination of a truck and trailer with 7 axles on Ohio highways without a permit?

A. ▢ 120,000 pounds

B. ▢ 122,000 pounds

C. ▢ 124,000 pounds

D. ▢ 126,000 pounds

15. What is the maximum allowable weight for a combination of a truck and trailer with 6 axles on Ohio highways without a permit?

A. ▢ 110,000 pounds

B. ▢ 112,000 pounds

C. ▢ 114,000 pounds

D. ▢ 116,000 pounds

Correct answers for vehicle size and weight limits exam 4

1. **C.** 105 feet

2. **B.** 45 feet

3. **B.** 74,000 pounds

4. **A.** 102,000 pounds

5. **B.** 14 feet

6. **C.** 18,000 pounds

7. **C.** 50 feet

8. **B.** 84,000 pounds

9. **B.** 80,000 pounds

10. **B.** 64,000 pounds

11. **B.** 50,000 pounds

12. **A.** 36,000 pounds

13. **C.** 52,000 pounds

14. **A.** 120,000 pounds

15. **B.** 112,000 pounds

Vehicle size and weight limits exam 5

1. **What is the maximum weight limit for a single axle of a tractor truck traveling on US highways?**

   A. ▢ 20,000 pounds

   B. ▢ 22,000 pounds

   C. ▢ 24,000 pounds

   D. ▢ 25,000 pounds

2. **What is the maximum weight limit for a vehicle with five axles traveling on US highways?**

   A. ▢ 67,000 pounds

   B. ▢ 72,000 pounds

   C. ▢ 77,000 pounds

   D. ▢ 82,000 pounds

3. **What is the maximum width allowed for a vehicle traveling on US interstates?**

   A. ▢ 8 feet

   B. ▢ 10 feet

   C. ▢ 12 feet

   D. ▢ 14 feet

4. **What is the maximum length allowed for a combination of three vehicles traveling on US highways?**

   A. ▢ 80 feet

   B. ▢ 85 feet

   C. ▢ 90 feet

D. ☐ 95 feet

5. **What is the maximum weight limit for a vehicle with seven axles traveling on US highways?**

A. ☐ 90,000 pounds

B. ☐ 95,000 pounds

C. ☐ 100,000 pounds

D. ☐ 105,000 pounds

6. **What is the maximum width allowed for a vehicle traveling on US interstates?**

A. ☐ 8 feet

B. ☐ 10 feet

C. ☐ 12 feet

D. ☐ 14 feet

7. **What is the maximum weight limit for a vehicle with eight axles traveling on US highways?**

A. ☐ 110,000 pounds

B. ☐ 120,000 pounds

C. ☐ 130,000 pounds

D. ☐ 140,000 pounds

8. **What is the maximum weight limit for a combination of two vehicles with five axles each traveling on US highways?**

A. ☐ 80,000 pounds

B. ☐ 90,000 pounds

C. ☐ 100,000 pounds

D. ▢ 110,000 pounds

9. **What is the maximum length limit for vehicles traveling on US highways?**

A. ▢ 50 feet

B. ▢ 60 feet

C. ▢ 70 feet

D. ▢ 80 feet

10. **What is the maximum height limit for vehicles traveling on US highways?**

A. ▢ 12 feet 6 inches

B. ▢ 13 feet 6 inches

C. ▢ 14 feet

D. ▢ 14 feet 6 inches

11. **What is the maximum weight limit for a combination of two vehicles with three axles each traveling on US interstates?**

A. ▢ 80,000 pounds

B. ▢ 86,000 pounds

C. ▢ 92,000 pounds

D. ▢ 98,000 pounds

12. **What is the maximum weight limit for a vehicle with two axles traveling on US highways?**

A. ▢ 34,000 pounds

B. ▢ 36,000 pounds

C. ▢ 38,000 pounds

D. ▢ 40,000 pounds

13. **What is the maximum weight limit for a combination of three vehicles with two axles each traveling on US highways?**

A. ▢ 70,000 pounds

B. ▢ 76,000 pounds

C. ▢ 80,000 pounds

D. ▢ 86,000 pounds

14. **What is the maximum length limit for a combination of two vehicles with two units each traveling on US highways?**

A. ▢ 55 feet

B. ▢ 60 feet

C. ▢ 65 feet

D. ▢ 70 feet

15. **What is the maximum weight limit for a standard Class C driver's license in most states in the United States?**

A. ▢ 6,000 pounds

B. ▢ 8,000 pounds

C. ▢ 10,000 pounds

D. ▢ 12,000 pounds

Correct answers for vehicle size and weight limits exam 5

1. **D.** 25,000 pounds
2. **B.** 72,000 pounds
3. **C.** 12 feet
4. **B.** 85 feet
5. **B.** 95,000 pounds
6. **D.** 14 feet
7. **B.** 120,000 pounds
8. **B.** 90,000 pounds
9. **B.** 60 feet
10. **B.** 13 feet 6 inches
11. **B.** 86,000 pounds
12. **D.** 40,000 pounds
13. **B.** 76,000 pounds
14. **B.** 60 feet
15. **C.** 10,000 pounds

Public transportation

Public transportation is an essential part of modern society, providing millions of people with a safe, affordable, and environmentally-friendly way to get around. In Ohio, public transportation is regulated by the Ohio Department of Transportation (ODOT), which is responsible for overseeing the state's public transit systems, including buses, trains, and other forms of transportation.

One of the most important aspects of public transportation is ensuring that drivers are properly trained and licensed to operate these vehicles. For this reason, the Ohio DMV has established a set of requirements that must be met in order to obtain a commercial driver's license (CDL) for operating public transit vehicles.

The Ohio DMV exam for public transportation is a comprehensive test that covers a wide range of topics related to safe driving and the operation of public transit vehicles. This exam is designed to test the knowledge, skills, and abilities of prospective public transit drivers, and is essential for ensuring the safety of passengers and other motorists on the road.

Some of the topics covered on the Ohio DMV exam for public transportation include driving laws and regulations, safe driving practices, vehicle inspection and maintenance, emergency procedures, and passenger safety. In addition to these topics, drivers must also demonstrate their ability to operate large vehicles, navigate through traffic, and respond quickly to emergency situations.

Preparing for the Ohio DMV exam for public transportation requires a significant amount of study and practice. Prospective drivers must become familiar with the rules and regulations of public transit driving, as well as the specific requirements of the vehicles they will be operating.

It is also important for drivers to develop their skills through hands-on training and practice, under the guidance of experienced instructors. By completing a comprehensive training program and passing the Ohio DMV exam for public transportation, drivers can help ensure the safety and reliability of Ohio's public transit systems for years to come.

For training purposes, you can mark the ▢ symbol next to what you think is the correct answer: Once you have chosen the correct answer, use a pencil or pen to mark the ▢ symbol next to that answer.

Public transportation exam

1. **Which public transportation system serves the Columbus metropolitan area?**

   A. ▢ Greater Dayton Regional Transit Authority

   B. ▢ Cincinnati Metro

   C. ▢ Greater Cleveland Regional Transit Authority

   D. ▢ Central Ohio Transit Authority

2. **Which Ohio city has a bus rapid transit system known as the HealthLine?**

   A. ▢ Cleveland

   B. ▢ Toledo

   C. ▢ Akron

   D. ▢ Youngstown

3. **Which of the following is a common challenge faced by Ohio public transportation systems?**

   A. ▢ Lack of ridership

   B. ▢ Lack of parking

   C. ▢ Lack of traffic

   D. ▢ Lack of road infrastructure

4. **Which Ohio public transportation system operates the Cincy EZRide shuttle service?**

   A. ▢ Central Ohio Transit Authority

   B. ▢ Greater Cleveland Regional Transit Authority

   C. ▢ Southwest Ohio Regional Transit Authority

   D. ▢ Greater Dayton Regional Transit Authority

5. **Which of the following modes of public transportation does the Stark Area Regional Transit Authority not operate?**

A. ▢ Buses

B. ▢ Trolleys

C. ▢ Trains

D. ▢ Vans

6. **Which of the following is a benefit of using public transportation in Ohio?**

A. ▢ Reduced air pollution

B. ▢ Increased traffic congestion

C. ▢ Higher transportation costs

D. ▢ More personal space

7. **What is the name of the public transportation system in Akron?**

A. ▢ Metro

B. ▢ COTA

C. ▢ RTA

D. ▢ SORTA

8. **Which Ohio city has a bike share program called CoGo?**

A. ▢ Cincinnati

B. ▢ Cleveland

C. ▢ Columbus

D. ▢ Dayton

9. **Which of the following modes of public transportation does the Portage Area Regional Transportation Authority not operate?**

A. ☐ Buses

B. ☐ Trolleys

C. ☐ Trains

D. ☐ Vans

10. **What type of public transportation system does the Toledo Area Regional Transit Authority operate?**

A. ☐ Buses

B. ☐ Trains

C. ☐ Ferries

D. ☐ Cable Cars

11. **What is the name of the public transportation system in Dayton?**

A. ☐ Metro

B. ☐ COTA

C. ☐ SORTA

D. ☐ RTA

12. **Which Ohio city has a public transportation system called the Metro Breeze?**

A. ☐ Toledo

B. ☐ Akron

C. ☐ Cincinnati

D. ☐ Cleveland

13. **Which of the following fare payment methods is accepted on the Greater Dayton Regional Transit Authority?**

A. ▢ Cash

B. ▢ Credit Card

C. ▢ Mobile Ticketing

D. ▢ All of the above

14. What type of public transportation system does the LakeTran system operate?

A. ▢ Buses

B. ▢ Train

C. ▢ Trolleys

D. ▢ Ferries

15. What is the name of the public transportation system in Cleveland?

A. ▢ Metro

B. ▢ COTA

C. ▢ SORTA

D. ▢ GCRTA

Correct answers for public transportation exam

1. **D.** Central Ohio Transit Authority

2. **A.** Cleveland

3. **A.** Lack of ridership

4. **C.** Southwest Ohio Regional Transit Authority

5. **C.** Trains

6. **A.** Reduced air pollution

7. **C.** RTA

8. **C.** Columbus

9. **C.** Trains

10. **A.** Buses

11. **A.** Metro

12. **B.** Akron

13. **D.** All of the above

14. **A.** Buses

15. **D.** GCRTA

Public transportation exam 2

1. **What is the name of the public transportation system serving Cleveland and Cuyahoga County?**

A. ▢ Greater Dayton RTA

B. ▢ Greater Cleveland RTA

C. ▢ Metro Regional Transit Authority

D. ▢ Central Ohio Transit Authority

2. **Which public transportation system serves the city of Cincinnati and its suburbs?**

A. ▢ Greater Dayton RTA

B. ▢ SORTA

C. ▢ COTA

D. ▢ Metro RTA

3. **What type of vehicles are used for public transportation in Ohio?**

A. ▢ Buses only

B. ▢ Trains only

C. ▢ Buses and trains

D. ▢ Cars and trucks

4. **Which public transportation system serves the city of Columbus and its suburbs?**

A. ▢ Metro RTA

B. ▢ COTA

C. ▢ SORTA

D. ▢ Greater Cleveland RTA

5. **What is the name of the public transportation system serving the city of Dayton and Montgomery County?**

A. ▢ COTA

B. ▢ Greater Dayton RTA

C. ▢ SORTA

D. ▢ Metro RTA

6. **How is public transportation in Ohio typically funded?**

A. ▢ Through user fees only

B. ▢ Through taxes only

C. ▢ Through a combination of user fees and taxes

D. ▢ Through private donations

7. **Which of the following is a benefit of using public transportation in Ohio?**

A. ▢ It is always faster than driving

B. ▢ It is more expensive than driving

C. ▢ It helps reduce air pollution

D. ▢ It is only available during certain times of day

8. **What is the name of the public transportation system serving the city of Toledo and surrounding areas?**

A. ▢ Greater Dayton RTA

B. ▢ Metro RTA

C. ▢ SORTA

D. ▢ TARTA

9. **Which of the following is not a common type of public transportation in Ohio?**

A. ▢ Buses

B. ▢ Trains

C. ▢ Ferries

D. ▢ Bicycles

10. **What is the name of the public transportation system serving the city of Akron and Summit County?**

A. ▢ SORTA

B. ▢ COTA

C. ▢ Metro RTA

D. ▢ METRO Bus and Vanpool

11. **What is the name of the public transportation system serving the city of Youngstown and Mahoning County?**

A. ▢ Metro RTA

B. ▢ SORTA

C. ▢ WRTA

D. ▢ COTA

12. **Which of the following is a common fare payment method for Ohio public transportation?**

A. ▢ Credit card only

B. ▢ Cash only

C. ▢ Contactless payment and cash

D. ▢ Online payment only

13. **What is the name of the light rail system serving the city of Cleveland and its suburbs?**

A. ▢ Cleveland Streetcar

B. ▢ Greater Cleveland RTA

C. ▢ Red Line

D. ▢ Blue Line

14. Which of the following is a common challenge faced by Ohio public transportation systems?

A. ▢ Lack of funding

B. ▢ Lack of ridership

C. ▢ Lack of vehicles

D. ▢ Lack of drivers

15. Which of the following is a benefit of using public transportation in Ohio?

A. ▢ It is always cheaper than driving

B. ▢ It helps reduce traffic congestion

C. ▢ It is only available during rush hour

D. ▢ It is always faster than driving

Correct answers for public transportation exam 2

1. **B.** Greater Cleveland RTA

2. **B.** SORTA

3. **C.** Buses and trains

4. **B.** COTA

5. **B.** Greater Dayton RTA

6. **C.** Through a combination of user fees and taxes

7. **C.** It helps reduce air pollution

8. **D.** TARTA

9. **C.** Ferries

10. **C.** Metro RTA

11. **C.** WRTA

12. **C.** Contactless payment and cash

13. **C.** Red Line

14. **A.** Lack of funding

15. **B.** It helps reduce traffic congestion

Public transportation exam 3

1. Which of the following public transportation systems serves the city of Akron and surrounding areas?

   A. □ SORTA

   B. □ TARTA

   C. □ COTA

   D. □ METRO Bus and Vanpool

2. Which public transportation system serves the city of Dayton and surrounding areas?

   A. □ Greater Dayton RTA

   B. □ Metro RTA

   C. □ SORTA

   D. □ WRTA

3. Which of the following is a type of service offered by some Ohio public transportation systems for people with disabilities?

   A. □ Paratransit

   B. □ Uber

   C. □ Taxi service

   D. □ Car rental

4. Which of the following public transportation systems serves the city of Toledo and surrounding areas?

   A. □ Greater Dayton RTA

   B. □ Metro RTA

   C. □ SORTA

D. ☐ TARTA

5. **What is the name of the bus rapid transit system serving Cleveland and the surrounding areas?**

A. ☐ Cleveland Streetcar

B. ☐ Blue Line

C. ☐ HealthLine

D. ☐ Red Line

6. **Which of the following is a common reason people in Ohio choose to use public transportation?**

A. ☐ It is always faster than driving

B. ☐ It is more convenient than driving

C. ☐ It is always cheaper than driving

D. ☐ It is more comfortable than driving

7. **Which of the following is a common way to access information about Ohio public transportation systems?**

A. ☐ Social media

B. ☐ Telephone

C. ☐ Websites

D. ☐ All of the above

8. **Which of the following is a type of public transportation service provided by the Toledo Area Regional Transit Authority (TARTA)?**

A. ☐ Paratransit

B. ☐ Bikeshare

C. ☐ Car rental

D. ☐ Uber

9. **Which of the following is a benefit of using public transportation in Ohio?**

A. ▢ It is always more expensive than driving

B. ▢ It always provides door-to-door service

C. ▢ It helps reduce air pollution

D. ▢ It is always faster than driving

10. **Which of the following public transportation systems serves the city of Akron and surrounding areas?**

A. ▢ Greater Dayton RTA

B. ▢ Metro RTA

C. ▢ SORTA

D. ▢ METRO Bus and Vanpool

11. **What is the name of the public transportation system in Cleveland, Ohio?**

A. ▢ GoBus

B. ▢ Greater Cleveland Regional Transit Authority (RTA)

C. ▢ Southwest Ohio Regional Transit Authority (SORTA)

D. ▢ Metro Regional Transit Authority (METRO)

12. **What is the cost of a single ride on the Central Ohio Transit Authority (COTA) bus system in Columbus, Ohio?**

A. ▢ $1.50

B. ▢ $2.00

C. ▢ $2.50

D. ▢ $3.00

13. Which public transportation system provides service to the Greater Cincinnati area in Ohio?

A. ▢ Toledo Area Regional Transit Authority (TARTA)

B. ▢ Akron Metro Regional Transit Authority (Metro RTA)

C. ▢ Miami Valley Regional Transit Authority (RTA)

D. ▢ Southwest Ohio Regional Transit Authority (SORTA)

14. What is the name of the public transportation system in Dayton, Ohio?

A. ▢ Laketran

B. ▢ Stark Area Regional Transit Authority (SARTA)

C. ▢ Greater Dayton Regional Transit Authority (GDRTA)

D. ▢ Athens Public Transit

15. Which public transportation system provides service to the city of Toledo in Ohio?

A. ▢ Toledo Area Regional Transit Authority (TARTA)

B. ▢ Greater Dayton Regional Transit Authority (GDRTA)

C. ▢ Central Ohio Transit Authority (COTA)

D. ▢ Metro Regional Transit Authority (METRO)

Correct answers for public transportation exam 3

1. **D.** METRO Bus and Vanpool

2. **A.** Greater Dayton RTA

3. **A.** Paratransit

4. **D.** TARTA

5. **C.** HealthLine

6. **B.** It is more convenient than driving

7. **D.** All of the above

8. **A.** Paratransit

9. **C.** It helps reduce air pollution

10. **D.** METRO Bus and Vanpool

11. **B.** Greater Cleveland Regional Transit Authority (RTA)

12. **B.** $2.00

13. **D.** Southwest Ohio Regional Transit Authority (SORTA)

14. **C.** Greater Dayton Regional Transit Authority (GDRTA)

15. **A.** Toledo Area Regional Transit Authority (TARTA)

Public transportation exam 4

1. **What is the name of the public transportation system that serves the city of Youngstown, Ohio?**

   A. ▢ Southwest Ohio Regional Transit Authority (SORTA)

   B. ▢ Laketran

   C. ▢ Stark Area Regional Transit Authority (SARTA)

   D. ▢ Metro Regional Transit Authority (METRO)

2. **Which of the following public transportation systems serves the city of Columbus, Ohio?**

   A. ▢ Miami Valley Regional Transit Authority (RTA)

   B. ▢ Central Ohio Transit Authority (COTA)

   C. ▢ Laketran

   D. ▢ Akron Metro Regional Transit Authority (Metro RTA)

3. **What is the name of the public transportation system that provides service to the Dayton International Airport?**

   A. ▢ Greater Dayton Regional Transit Authority (GDRTA)

   B. ▢ Cleveland Regional Transit Authority (RTA)

   C. ▢ Stark Area Regional Transit Authority (SARTA)

   D. ▢ Miami Valley Regional Transit Authority (RTA)

4. **What is the name of the public transportation system that provides service to the Akron-Canton Airport in Ohio?**

   A. ▢ Akron Metro Regional Transit Authority (Metro RTA)

   B. ▢ Laketran

   C. ▢ Stark Area Regional Transit Authority (SARTA)

D. ▢ Central Ohio Transit Authority (COTA)

5. Which of the following public transportation systems serves the city of Lima, Ohio?

A. ▢ Toledo Area Regional Transit Authority (TARTA)

B. ▢ Laketran

C. ▢ Metro Regional Transit Authority (METRO)

D. ▢ Lima Allen County Regional Transit Authority (LACRTA)

6. What is the name of the public transportation system that serves the city of Mansfield, Ohio?

A. ▢ Miami Valley Regional Transit Authority (RTA)

B. ▢ Mansfield/Richland County Public Transit

C. ▢ Greater Dayton Regional Transit Authority (GDRTA)

D. ▢ Central Ohio Transit Authority (COTA)

7. Which of the following public transportation systems serves the city of Canton, Ohio?

A. ▢ Miami Valley Regional Transit Authority (RTA)

B. ▢ Metro Regional Transit Authority (METRO)

C. ▢ Greater Cleveland Regional Transit Authority (RTA)

D. ▢ Stark Area Regional Transit Authority (SARTA)

8. Which of the following Ohio public transportation systems operates a trolleybus system?

A. ▢ Toledo Area Regional Transit Authority (TARTA)

B. ▢ Greater Dayton Regional Transit Authority (GDRTA)

C. ▢ Central Ohio Transit Authority (COTA)

D. ▢ Cleveland Regional Transit Authority (RTA)

9. **What is the name of the public transportation system that serves the city of Sandusky, Ohio?**

A. ▢ Sandusky Transit System

B. ▢ Athens Public Transit

C. ▢ Southwest Ohio Regional Transit Authority (SORTA)

D. ▢ Greater Dayton Regional Transit Authority (GDRTA)

10. **Which Ohio public transportation system provides paratransit services for individuals with disabilities in the Columbus area?**

A. ▢ Laketran

B. ▢ Central Ohio Transit Authority (COTA)

C. ▢ Stark Area Regional Transit Authority (SARTA)

D. ▢ Toledo Area Regional Transit Authority (TARTA)

11. **Which of the following public transportation systems serves the city of Zanesville, Ohio?**

A. ▢ Greater Dayton Regional Transit Authority (GDRTA)

B. ▢ Athens Public Transit

C. ▢ Stark Area Regional Transit Authority (SARTA)

D. ▢ Muskingum County Transit Co.

12. **What is the name of the public transportation system that serves the city of Marietta, Ohio?**

A. ▢ Stark Area Regional Transit Authority (SARTA)

B. ▢ Laketran

C. ▢ Marietta Transit

D. ▢ Greater Dayton Regional Transit Authority (GDRTA)

13. **Which of the following Ohio public transportation systems operates a light rail system?**

A. ▢ Metro Regional Transit Authority (METRO)

B. ▢ Greater Cleveland Regional Transit Authority (RTA)

C. ▢ Toledo Area Regional Transit Authority (TARTA)

D. ▢ Central Ohio Transit Authority (COTA)

14. Which of the following public transportation systems provides service to the city of Portsmouth, Ohio?

A. ▢ Athens Public Transit

B. ▢ Stark Area Regional Transit Authority (SARTA)

C. ▢ Greater Dayton Regional Transit Authority (GDRTA)

D. ▢ Scioto County Transit

15. What is the name of the public transportation system that serves the city of Steubenville, Ohio?

A. ▢ Steubenville Transit System

B. ▢ Athens Public Transit

C. ▢ Stark Area Regional Transit Authority (SARTA)

D. ▢ Jefferson County Regional Transit Authority (JCRTA)

Correct answers for public transportation exam 4

1. **D.** Metro Regional Transit Authority (METRO)

2. **B.** Central Ohio Transit Authority (COTA)

3. **A.** Greater Dayton Regional Transit Authority (GDRTA)

4. **C.** Stark Area Regional Transit Authority (SARTA)

5. **D.** Lima Allen County Regional Transit Authority (LACRTA)

6. **B.** Mansfield/Richland County Public Transit

7. **D.** Stark Area Regional Transit Authority (SARTA)

8. **D.** Cleveland Regional Transit Authority (RTA)

9. **A.** Sandusky Transit System

10. **B.** Central Ohio Transit Authority (COTA)

11. **D.** Muskingum County Transit Co.

12. **C.** Marietta Transit

13. **B.** Greater Cleveland Regional Transit Authority (RTA)

14. **D.** Scioto County Transit

15. **D.** Jefferson County Regional Transit Authority (JCRTA)

Public transportation exam 5

1. **Which public transportation system serves Cleveland and the surrounding suburbs?**

   A. ▢ Greater Dayton Regional Transit Authority

   B. ▢ Central Ohio Transit Authority

   C. ▢ Greater Cleveland Regional Transit Authority

   D. ▢ Toledo Area Regional Transit Authority

2. **What is the name of the streetcar system that operates in Cincinnati?**

   A. ▢ MetroLink

   B. ▢ The Cincinnati Bell Connector

   C. ▢ Ohio Streetcar

   D. ▢ Buckeye Express

3. **Which of the following cities is not served by the Southwest Ohio Regional Transit Authority?**

   A. ▢ Cincinnati

   B. ▢ Dayton

   C. ▢ Hamilton

   D. ▢ Middletown

4. **What type of public transportation system is the Portage Area Regional Transportation Authority?**

   A. ▢ Bus

   B. ▢ Streetcar

   C. ▢ Subway

   D. ▢ Ferry

5. **Which public transportation system serves the capital city of Ohio?**

A. ◻ Greater Cleveland Regional Transit Authority

B. ◻ Central Ohio Transit Authority

C. ◻ Metro Regional Transit Authority

D. ◻ Southeastern Ohio Regional Transit Authority

6. **What is the name of the light rail system that serves the city of Cleveland?**

A. ◻ Red Line

B. ◻ Blue Line

C. ◻ Green Line

D. ◻ Orange Line

7. **Which public transportation system serves the city of Akron?**

A. ◻ Akron Metro Regional Transit Authority

B. ◻ Greater Dayton Regional Transit Authority

C. ◻ Portage Area Regional Transportation Authority

D. ◻ Greater Cleveland Regional Transit Authority

8. **What is the name of the bus rapid transit system that serves the city of Cleveland?**

A. ◻ The Rapid

B. ◻ MetroLink

C. ◻ The Busway

D. ◻ The Flyer

9. **What is the primary mode of public transportation in Ohio?**

A. ▢ Buses

B. ▢ Trains

C. ▢ Boats

D. ▢ Planes

10. Which Ohio city has a light rail system?

A. ▢ Cincinnati

B. ▢ Columbus

C. ▢ Dayton

D. ▢ Cleveland

11. What is the name of the public transportation system in Cincinnati?

A. ▢ Metro

B. ▢ COTA

C. ▢ RTA

D. ▢ TARTA

12. What type of public transportation does the Greater Dayton Regional Transit Authority operate?

A. ▢ Buses

B. ▢ Trains

C. ▢ Trolleys

D. ▢ Ferries

13. Which Ohio city has a streetcar system?

A. ▢ Columbus

B. ▢ Cincinnati

C. ▢ Cleveland

D. ▢ Akron

14. **Which of the following is not a type of fare payment accepted on the Greater Cleveland Regional Transit Authority?**

A. ▢ Cash

B. ▢ Credit Card

C. ▢ Mobile Ticketing

D. ▢ Personal Check

15. **How many public transportation systems are there in Ohio?**

A. ▢ 3

B. ▢ 5

C. ▢ 7

D. ▢ 9

Correct answers for public transportation exam 5

1. **C.** Greater Cleveland Regional Transit Authority

2. **B.** The Cincinnati Bell Connector

3. **B.** Dayton

4. **A.** Bus

5. **B.** Central Ohio Transit Authority

6. **A.** Red Line

7. **A.** Akron Metro Regional Transit Authority

8. **A.** The Rapid

9. **A.** Buses

10. **D.** Cleveland

11. **A.** Metro

12. **A.** Buses

13. **B.** Cincinnati

14. **D.** Personal Check

15. **B.** 5

Conclusion

In conclusion, the Ohio DMV Exam Workbook is an essential guide to help prepare for the Ohio driving test. With its comprehensive coverage of the state's driving rules and regulations, this workbook provides a clear and concise guide to the information necessary to pass the driving test.

Throughout the book, readers are introduced to the various aspects of driving in Ohio, including traffic signs, rules of the road, and defensive driving techniques. Additionally, the workbook offers a range of practice tests, allowing readers to test their knowledge and identify areas where they need to improve.

The Ohio DMV Exam Workbook is written in a clear and accessible style, making it easy for readers to understand the information. The book is also well-organized, with each section building on the previous one so that readers can develop a comprehensive understanding of Ohio's driving rules and regulations.

One of the most valuable features of the Ohio DMV Exam Workbook is its range of practice tests. These tests are designed to mimic the Ohio driving test, giving readers a realistic experience of what to expect on exam day. By taking these tests, readers can identify areas where they need to focus their studying and can become more confident in their ability to pass the driving test.

Another critical aspect of the Ohio DMV Exam Workbook is its emphasis on defensive driving techniques. This section of the book provides valuable information on how to anticipate and avoid potential hazards on the road, making it an essential read for anyone serious about becoming a safe and responsible driver.

The Ohio DMV Exam Workbook is a must-read for anyone preparing to take the Ohio driving test. Its clear and concise information, practical advice, and range of practice tests provide readers with everything they need to know to pass the test and become safe and responsible drivers.

However, it is essential to note that while the Ohio DMV Exam Workbook is an excellent resource, other resources should be used to prepare for the driving test. It is also essential to practice driving with a licensed driver and to review the Ohio driver's manual, which provides more in-depth information on the state's driving rules and regulations.

In addition, it is essential to remember that passing the driving test is just the beginning of a driver's journey. Safe and responsible driving requires ongoing practice, vigilance, and a commitment to following the road rules. Using the Ohio DMV Exam Workbook as a foundation, readers can develop the knowledge and skills they need to become safe and responsible drivers for life.

In conclusion, the Ohio DMV Exam Workbook is an essential guide for anyone preparing to take the Ohio driving test. Its comprehensive coverage of the state's driving rules and regulations, practical advice, and range of practice tests provides readers with everything they need to know to pass the test and become safe and responsible drivers. While it is important to remember that passing the driving test is just the beginning of a driver's journey, the Ohio DMV Exam Workbook provides an excellent foundation for developing the knowledge and skills necessary to become a safe and responsible driver for life.